ACQUISITIONS
DISCARDED
P9-ELH-487

3-23-77

A CHURCH WITHOUT WALLS

A CHURCH WITHOUT WALLS

Odin K. Stenberg

DIMENSION BOOKS
BETHANY FELLOWSHIP, INC.
Minneapolis, Minnesota

A Church Without Walls
by Odin K. Stenberg

Library of Congress Catalog Card Number:
76-7702

ISBN 0-87123-056-9

Copyright © 1976
Bethany Fellowship, Inc.
All Rights Reserved

DIMENSION BOOKS
Published by Bethany Fellowship, Inc.
6820 Auto Club Road
Minneapolis, Minnesota 55438

Printed in the United States of America

1963721

To the memory of my father,
who dreamed of writing a book
about the Christian faith.

ODIN STENBERG is a native of North Dakota. He served with the merchant marine during the Second World War. Following his term of service he received a B.A. from the University of Washington and a degree in theology from Luther Theological Seminary.

His involvements have been varied: He directed a student center in Japan, developed a visual-conversational seminar series for Christian instruction in Brazil, and taught both elementary and secondary school on the West Coast. Prior to writing *A Church Without Walls* he authored *A Review of Redemption* and *Crossing Borders,* as well as articles for periodicals.

Mr. Stenberg is currently directing a retreat center in Amery, Wisconsin.

How It Comes Together

If you wanted to get something going in Wittenberg, you put it up for debate in some customary place. So when an angry young monk nailed his ninety-five arguments to the cathedral door, he was merely inviting his friends and colleagues to come together to kick those things around. He wanted to challenge the status quo, to ventilate feelings and explore the situations where changes could be made.

Once again there is a call for the catalyst. I would like to see all kinds of people sitting down in the college lounges, in sidewalk cafes, in union halls, to vent their frustrations and talk about the possibilities of renewal in the Christian community. The original reformation brought a wonderful infusion of new life. I believe the same thing can happen where perceptive men and women will consider the return to "A Church Without Walls."

I think many will agree that there is a depressing "deadness" today in places that were once alive and exciting. Looking around us, we find that many of the churches are plagued with a kind of mental paralysis. Stuck in all kinds of ruts, with modern and ornate buildings, but with stereotyped forms of operation and worship, they are somehow unable to effect the fundamental changes that would make them relevant in the world of today.

We are faced with an overpowering affair that has calcified into a sort of caste system of "clergy" and "laity." It is fragmented into a bewildering array of denominations, and yet we go on taking for granted that this is the only proper formulation of the Church! Have we stopped to consider that all this could be quite a radical departure from nearly everything that the Church of our Lord is intended to be? We may wonder what has happened to the simple and dynamic pattern of Christian community that was born at Pentecost, a church unencumbered by the "walls" that separate clergy from laity, and Baptist from Lutheran.

It will be the purpose of this book to join hands with the growing number who are genuinely concerned about reform and renewal. It will seek to zero in on practical areas of church life and project the need of change in some of the customs we may never have questioned. Each chapter will center on a familiar problem and suggest an alternative in harmony with New Testament principles. If this appears to be negative, please note that the dream reaching for fulfillment is totally positive!

You, the reader, will be aware of recurring themes. You will sense a concern for a generation groping for an experience of community that is not generally available. Moving from the satirical to the constructive, I trust you will be caught up in the glad awareness of what the Church of Jesus really is. I invite you to a recovery of "A Church Without Walls" that can restore to our time the vital Christian community that once was and shall be again.

Odin K. Stenberg

Issues of Our Time

1

Have we been
Knocking at the Wrong Door?

Becky's letter brought her into focus as if she had been standing there beside me—tall, attractive and open-hearted. I was amused at her burn-all-the-bridges intensity and yet I felt sympathetic.

Becky had been my "right hand" when I was the principal of a Christian elementary school in Los Angeles. Lacking the money to hire a secretary, I was delighted to have her pop her head into my office practically every morning after she had let her daughter off for school. Always the smile and the question—"Anything I can do for you today?"

And invariably there was. A stack of letters to type, some filing to do, or perhaps a run to the stationery store. I don't know what I would have done without her.

Becky was a fairly new convert to the Christian faith, constantly alert to any way at all to serve the Lord. Her husband was a hod carrier with a construction crew. The work was irregular, and there were frequent bouts with the bottle, but there was never a hint of the hardship that dogged her life. If I offered a few dollars for her help, she was downright offended.

Eventually things got so bad, the family finances so low, that Becky had to go to work. Happily she found a job as a parish worker in a small church in another part of the city. Meanwhile my family and I moved on to a new assignment in Brazil, and on this particular morning came one of her many letters. She began by telling of a "rally Sunday" they had planned.

Island of Angelinos

The church where Becky worked was a small island of German descendants in a vast ocean of black and chicano Angelinos. The pastor had resolved to make this a "mission church" by going after everyone regardless of creed or color.

Full of enthusiasm, Becky had ventured out to ring doorbells, inviting the people of the neighborhood to the rally Sunday. When the big day dawned Becky stood at the door to welcome the new arrivals. The regulars came straggling in, but where were the new faces? She had stood at the door of over a hundred homes, flashed her bright smile and made her little speech. Now the moment of truth, not a single one had responded!

That night she took out her portable typewriter and poured out her utter dejection. "I don't know what to do," she said. "I've failed my church. I have let the pastor down. I'm a total failure." She spoke of quitting her job and looking for something else.

Priceless Pearl

As soon as I could find the time I sat down and hurried off a reply. "Becky, dear lady, I know how you feel because I've been through it myself. But it isn't all that bad! You are learning what it means to be a part of the Christian mission.

"You have a priceless pearl to give away to people so blind they can't see what it's worth. You have Good News to share with a world that couldn't care less, but isn't this what it's all about?

"Now you can get down to business. How about getting to know just one or two of these families who live near the church? Even though they are turned off to religion, you will find they do have needs. And these may not be such obvious things as food or clothing for the kids. Chances are they will run deeper. Loneliness, frustration, or a feeling that nobody cares what happens to them.

"Whatever it is, Becky, when they discover that you are willing to listen, and you honestly want to reach out and help them fill the void with your love and friendship, they will begin to warm up to you. And the color of your skin won't make a bit of difference.

"They probably won't ask, 'Why do you bother yourself with us and our problems?' but it will be crossing their minds. And when this begins to happen you will have your first real chance to talk about the Kingdom, to let them know that you care because of the One who cares very much."

To Entice a Stranger

I don't know why it takes us so long to learn the limitations of the doorbell routine. Going from door to door to try to entice a total stranger to come to our particular church—is this evangelism, and was it ever? Isn't it more often an evasion, an escape from the much more demanding challenge of getting to know my neighbor, and from sitting down to share my faith with someone I already know perfectly well?

I wore out a lot of shoe leather, I got to know bone-weary discouragement and the bitter taste of defeat before I finally "wised up" to this. Becky's letter brought back the years when I had done the identical thing and had the same dismal results.

I remember one afternoon when I was going "door to door" in a small Japanese village, determined to call at every house and establishment on the street. In Japan you don't walk up to a house and press a doorbell. You push open a sliding door. Inside there is a rotating mechanism that raucously rings a bell as the door moves aside. Then you step into a sort of recessed porch called a "genkan" and announce yourself. The servant or the lady of the house will respond by opening the delicate interior "fusuma" about an inch. From that narrow vantage you are appraised and scrutinized as you introduce yourself and state your business.

And that's usually the end of it. The fusuma closes and you have been politely dismissed. Rarely ever do you get to take off your shoes and sit down on the "zabaton" for a chat and a cup of tea—unless you are a friend.

Screaming in Chorus

Some business places have the recessed "genkan" entrance, but do not have the inner wall of fusuma doors. They will have, instead, a string of short banners imprinted with the ancient character symbols that identify their particular line of business. Generally there will also be a sign outside, but I never was too expert at reading those ancient "kanji" characters, and especially not during those early years.

Already tired from pushing open dozens of doors, no longer very alert, I slid open another door and found myself standing beside a gathering of ladies entirely in the natural. One look at the paleface "gaijin" and they all screamed in chorus, grabbed their towels and made for the back door. I had walked into the ladies' section of the Public Bath!

I went away laughing, and when I thought of what I had been doing all day it seemed as ridiculous. I had rung my last doorbell! I would have to find some other way to tell my story, or abandon the venture altogether.

Limited Assets

I began to wonder what I could do for them that they could not do for themselves. What kind of practical help could I offer, a service that they would recognize as valid and desirable? Taking stock of my limited assets, I realized I could teach English, the language many of the Japanese very much wanted to learn as a utilitarian second language.

I had a bachelor apartment, actually just one large tatami room on the second floor of what had formerly been the servants' quarters in the courtyard of a wealthy patrician. Rendered penniless by the destruction of the business in the recent war, his widow existed by renting out these rooms.

One of my neighbors in the same cluster of shanties was Suzuki, a psychology professor in the community college. When I found that Suzuki Sensei shared the general interest in English, I invited him in for a cup of tea. He began to bring some of his students and we spent many a pleasant evening, often laughing at each other's mistakes—my mangling of the Japanese and their vowel hassles with the language of the Americans.

Contradictory Diagnosis

As the one concession to "missionary work" we agreed to use a modern translation of the New Testament as our text. A few of the students showed some interest and occasionally asked questions about Christianity. So did Suzuki, but his nominal Buddhist moorings and a deep Freudian bias made it hard for him to accept the "simple" teachings of Jesus. Especially to yield to His uncompromising claim to be the one way, the one truth, the one life.

After many months of classes my roster of converts still registered zero, but Suzuki, highly intelligent, had made substantial progress in English. And we had become friends.

One day he came by, very depressed, and told me his attractive young wife was gravely ill. Most marriages there were traditionally arranged by relatives as a matter of economic or social convenience; and "love," if there was any, was generally thought of as an unnecessary embarrassment.

Not so with Suzuki. He had chosen this woman himself, and he loved her dearly. Now he had consulted four different physicians and had gotten four contradictory diagnoses! None of the remedies worked. Seeing the color fade from her face and her life ebbing away, Suzuki was desperate. Even though he felt no motivation to accept Christianity, he saw no harm in my offering a prayer for her recovery.

I also contacted a local doctor, a Christian who was like a brother to me. He examined her and shook his head. He described an unfamiliar kind of internal infection, and told me it might be arrested by massive injections of penicillin, but he had little or none on hand. In those postwar years in an impoverished Japan, it was not available for general use.

I got in touch with an American doctor at a mission hospital in Tokyo. Sure enough, they had a supply. It came in the next mail, without charge, and Suzuki's wife began to respond.

Transfer to Tokyo

She was still a very sick lady when my mission transferred me to Tokyo to pioneer an approach to university students. I became totally immersed in the new assignment, so much so that Suzuki and his situation slipped almost entirely from my mind. There were so many new ones to be concerned about.

One evening, about two years later, I was surprised by a telephone call. It was Suzuki. He apologized for the lack of communication, and he had a request. He had been listening, he said, to a Christian radio broadcast. He had sent for their Bible instruction materials pointing the way to personal salvation. Now they had all been completed.

"Yes," he said, "my wife is well now . . . and I have come to believe in God. I have accepted Jesus. Will you arrange for my baptism?"

2

Dear Abby, do you know of
A Cure for Pew-Sitting?

I can think of two or three exciting experiments in church renewal. One would be the Circle Church in downtown Chicago. And another, the Church of the Savior in Washington, D.C., but even in these creative innovations there is an accent on clerical control. Stimulating as they are, it is rather interesting that much of what they do does not easily transplant into other settings. Generally speaking, when we take a candid look at what the churches are doing, and call it a "spectator" proposition, we are telling it like it is.

I suppose there are some who will insist that this is simply not so. "Not in *my* church! In my church, everybody is active."

Neatly Packaged

Everybody active? Let's see what the women are doing. Likely they will be expending a bit of energy on some kind of monthly coffee hour. There is, of course, the matter of finding a suitable recipe and stirring up a batch of goodies to put in the automatic oven. A few others will be vigorously dialing telephones to coordinate committees.

The task force of ladies will have no lack of commendable causes—world missions, parish education, and the like. But I wonder if there is much stimulus to native ability? In the liturgical churches, the customary devotional for the monthly meeting comes neatly packaged from headquarters.

In the face of self-diminishing roles, nothing so plainly reflects "the restlessness of the natives" as the push to get into the clergy. I think the women are saying, "Look, you guys, I'm tired of sitting here on Sunday morning! I'm not just a good-smelling mannequin down here. Let *me* have a piece of the platform, too. I've got something to say."

And of course they have! Yet the irony is that the growing trend to ordain women into the clergy merely underscores the confusion about the true ministry of the church.

Light Touch

The congregation's youth corps generally have their activity mapped out for them by the pastor, youth leader, or some parish couple volunteering their help. Characteristically there will be a light touch on the spiritual, and a heavy accent on the social, so that being there and being along will be "fun." On Sunday morning they are expected to sit and listen (and not be too obnoxious about it) until they are old enough to assume the burdens currently borne by their elders.

Heavy Logistics

The men are enlisted in the local shock troops to hand out Sunday bulletins, show the people where to sit and how to get out again without stampeding. Others are given the challenge to carry collection plates down the aisles, pass them across the pews, and bring them back to the altar again.

The more willing and ambitious male members are coaxed into accepting positions as church "officers." These meet once a month to weigh and ponder such heavy logistics as repairing the leak in the chancel roof, or widening the front sidewalk.

The overwhelming majority of the faithful find that their religion occupies them even less than this. They have been assured

and reassured that the crowning requirement for pleasing the Almighty is to attend
the church on Sunday. They are to "witness" to their more maverick neighbor by
backing the car out of the garage, every
Sunday at ten-thirty, and courageously
driving off to church! They are also aware
that the divine pleasure depends on giving
a little money, at least a dollar bill, so the
budget can be met and the preacher can
be paid.

Professional Religionist

Perhaps this is where the trouble begins.
If we understand that we are paying this
one professional religionist to put on a
weekly performance, replete with a twenty-
minute monologue, then it is a very short
hop to the happy conclusion that it is ex-
clusively his job to attend to everything
"spiritual"! But if a church member does
not find himself fully involved, either in
worship or in relating to those outside, what
then are the possibilities for internal
growth?

It comes as no great surprise that the
veteran pastor is finding it harder and harder to fill the vacancies in the church council,
the board of ushers and the other committees. I wonder if it has occurred to anyone that this may be encouraging! An in-

dication that the laity is beginning to recognize this kind of "busy work" for what it patently is. Not laywork at all, in any solid sense, but merely the housekeeping chores of the institutional church.

Demeaning Role

The problem with chores is that they tend to get monotonous. A new member usually comes into the church with a lot of enthusiasm for any little job the pastor may give him, but he doesn't need to be in the program for too many years to run the gamut of all possible assignments, and the whole thing gets to be a drag.

He begins to see all this as the "ghetto religion" that it actually is, and he turns his attention to golfing, fishing or other diversions. He gets involved in the civic organizations, where he is at any rate a peer, and where he *can* get to the top if he is so inclined! The life may be less fulfilling than what he once dreamed of in the church, but it will at least allow him to go beyond a demeaning secondary role.

Thin Theology

Can there be any doubt that we need to reconsider the quality of our Actor-Spectator theater? I would question that the resulting variety of bland belief is either building the Church of Jesus Christ or winning the world outside. It may, in fact, be robbing us of the very life and vitality He came to give.

The prophet Jeremiah spoke of a time when people would no longer be drinking from *a spring of living water* (as in the days of the early church) but would be building cisterns for themselves.[1] The trouble with the best of cisterns is that water gets stale when there is no outflow. And of course we don't recommend stagnant water to anyone!

I have a suspicion that spectator theology is a thin and stale theology. It is not unusual to fall into conversation with the typical church member and discover that the ideas he has carried away from the worship service (and the beliefs by which he actually lives) are based on a hodgepodge of misconceptions. And some of his firmly held beliefs may be shockingly unChristian.

What is gratifying about the current experiments in church renewal, such as the one David Mains has pioneered in the Circle Church, is what it tells about the growing awareness of the need to move from a spectator stance into a valid involvement that can embrace every believer. Happily there are better times ahead!

3

Do some things go together, like

The Heron and Rhinoceros?

One of the marvelous phenomena in God's creation is symbiosis, that indispensable relationship in which two organisms live together for the benefit of both. It describes a necessary affinity, a biological balance without which neither could achieve its ecological function and reach its normal productiveness. Common examples of this are the pollinating activity of the bees that enable the trees to bear fruit, and the little white heron that feeds on the ticks that plague the elephant and rhinoceros.

There is a parallel application of the symbiotic principle in the activity of the Spirit among believers. Much of the frustration which the parishioner may experience in his association with the church stems from the failure to recognize this principle, especially as it applies to the relationship between *witness* and *worship*. Let us look first at the problem involved in Christian witness, for if he is an "evangelical," the chances are that he faces a weekly bombardment with the "witness" theme. And he is being confronted with increasingly intensified programs of outreach.

Bootcamp Seminars

In a currently popular expression of this, the active core of the congregation is summoned into a massive battalion for motivation and indoctrination. From the moment of jetting into some strategic Fort Benning, the recruits are lectured and role-played in a "how to witness" curriculum. Immediately following these bootcamp seminars there is a feverish assault on human inertia that is calculated to set any town on fire and turn the country upside down.

It would be convenient if human rapport and response could be predicted and programmed into a neat "how to" package, but of course it can't. The campaign that began with the muster of troops and the fanfare is destined to peter out. And the typical sequel is a quiet disengaging and settling back into the security of the pew. There simply is no crash course by which a winsome witness can be accomplished.

Mutual Dependency

I think we need to recognize that spontaneous communication flows out of a deeply fulfilling sense of *worship*, the other essential element in a logical symbiosis. Worship and communication are linked in a mutual dependency. The believer who is not entrusted with a necessity to participate, actively, in the corporate worship of God will subsequently not trust himself to talk to the indifferent or the hostile about his faith.

The now-go-out-there-and-witness crescendo does not alter the reality that a superficial proximity to Christian worship—listening to sermons and repeating ancient or impromptu liturgies—can only leave a person unequipped and unready to receive or to say anything significant about religion and life. No matter how highly attested are the gimmicks he is given, he will not feel qualified to articulate his life with God unless he has been building up for this in a quality of worship experience where he is not a passive recipient, but where he is regularly vocalizing his convictions within the inner circle of those who love and encourage and correct.

We have an example of this love and correction in the delightful encounter with

Apollos in Ephesus.[2] Priscilla and Aquila must have enjoyed his fervor as he shared his new life with the Jews in the synagogue. And since they had so recently been in Paul's company, they took him into their home and opened up new vistas of truth and experience to enrich his ministry and enhance his effectiveness.

I suppose it can be the function of the clergy to nudge and motivate the laity to form the smaller groupings where actual involvement is possible, but I would question that they can be regularly present in any sustained endeavor to cultivate and discover the basics of adequate worship and fellowship. However profoundly he may wish to identify, the clergyman will confront the salient fact that the presence of a professional almost invariably inhibits to some degree. He can discreetly drop in, from time to time, but he must as carefully fade out and move on to another group, or the normal expression of the gifts of the Spirit may be stifled and suppressed.

Vital and Alive

What are the essential components of satisfying worship? Certainly a major element must be the teaching of the newly initiated, by the more mature, in the practical applications of the Word of God. In an atmosphere of mutual acceptance and out-going love, even the most timid feel free to participate. There is a spirit of prayer and praise and expectancy, both vocal and silent. In halting and eloquent speech, and in lyric and creative melody, there is a sharing of day-to-day experience, of lessons learned and needs expressed. Ultimately there will be the arresting of minds and emotions to enter into the suffering, the death, the resurrection, and the living presence of the Lord, our Brother, in the breaking of bread and the passing of the cup from one to the other.

Whether it be good or evil, isn't it still true that each of us will speak *out of the overflow of the heart*? [3] The very environment that nurtures individual growth will constitute the preparation for a natural imparting of what is vital and alive. When the Christian is inwardly conditioned and filled with the Spirit, he will need no gimmicks, and the settings for an essential sharing of the faith need not be structured. Don't we find that the most impressive communication often occurs in the casual situations that just "happen"?

Personal participation and total involvement in the worship experience is an inseparable prelude to all sharing of life and faith with the non-Christian world. The freshness and effervescence of a life newly born, and continually reborn, depends on this insoluble tie with fellow believers. And it almost equally impinges on a persistent outflow into the parched places of the wilderness outside.

1963721

4

Are we kidding ourselves about

A Special Kind of Magic?

A big rangy Dutchman came to the door and let me in, but he wasn't too happy to see me. In his mind I suppose I came on as a pesky sort of truant officer from the local church. And he would clearly have preferred not to be disturbed. He may have been a little embarrassed by the drink in his hand, and irritated that it should make any difference.

"Yah, I know I should be going to church," he said, and began trotting out the customary excuses. He liked being casual; hated to "dress up" and put on a tie. He didn't like to be stuck with a lot of stuffy, superficial people. Anyway the place was full of hypocrites . . .

I listened until he had run out of reasons, and then I said, "Why do you feel you should be going to church?"

He had been pacing the floor, and now he swung around, redfaced and angry. For a moment I thought he was going to hit me, or throw me out of the house.

"Why!" he said, "that's a fine thing for a man like you to ask!"

I just sat there and looked at him, and I said it again, "Well, what makes you think you should? Why bother yourself— if it's such a drag and a bore?"

Unwilling Witness

I had come because I had his son Jan in the parish school. Jan was a beautiful boy, a too-sober, pale-complexioned little face, thick wavy black hair. He resembled his mother who had formerly worked as a model. Obviously alert and intelligent, he was nevertheless failing in every subject. All the love and gentle coaxing of an able Christian teacher had left him unmoved. Finding that Jan had a mental block toward everything we were trying to do for him, I had finally spoken to his mother.

From her I learned that Jan's father was an instructor at the university, and that he tended to ignore the boy as though he were a part of the woodwork. Jan was the unwilling witness to many a violent quarrel between his mother and dad. And lately, instead of coming home, his father frequently spent his nights with a young widow in another part of the city.

I had come to the head of the house, primarily to get acquainted and to see if I could get him to work with us in reaching his son. I knew he would need to sense that he was accepted exactly as he was, without pretext or pre-conditions of any kind. And I prayed inwardly that I might be able to apply the particular therapy that the Spirit of Christ can provide.

I had my doubts that he would find the help he needed by going to any of the local churches. For him, in any case, this would not likely be the answer, and especially so because he held the common misconceptions about what the church is and what it is for. So I tried to clear away a little of the confusion.

Mysterious Virtue

One durable notion is that there is a quality of *magic*, a mysterious undefined sort of virtue, in the very act of "going to church"! Whether it is the occasional Christmas and Easter visit, or a sense of weekly obligation, this apparently goes unquestioned, even though opinions differ about what is accomplished by it all.

If a newspaper reporter was to move about with a microphone at the entrance to some church on a Sunday morning, and if the people were uninhibited enough to give candid answers, I believe the results would be rather predictable. Some would say they go for the sake of the kids, out of a sense of duty. Some would possibly admit they are on the alert for neighborhood business contacts. Others would quite honestly tell how they find it a restful, quieting thing to do. They enjoy listening to the pipe organ, singing the hymns, and look forward to meeting their friends.

The roving reporter would also meet the truly devout and believing who would say, "I come here to *get* something, especially from the message of the pastor. I feel the need to recharge my spiritual batteries for the long week in the nerve-wracking world outside the church."

A Shared Celebration

In general, the answers would likely reflect the vague sense that we are not as Christian as we ought to be, and that the church is the place to go to *become* Christian, or more so. But it is altogether too rare that anything like this happens.

On the other hand, what if we are dedicated Christians? And we have been given to understand that the crucial requirement is to go to some holy building, to sit in on a weekly performance, and serve on an occasional committee? We may need to discern that an association with a church that is out of touch with reality will be of little or no help to us.

What the church signifies, above all, is that here the gifts of teaching, of prayer and praise and the breaking of the bread, are to be a *shared* celebration. It implies a total participation. I would say that even the most committed Christian, who conceives of the church primarily as a place to go and "get something" for the inner life, is confused and unclear about what the Church is.

Invisible Altar

Is the Church, in fact, ever a "place"? Is it physically possible to "go to church" as the cliche implies? The Church may *gather*. It can come into being wherever two or three get together in the company of the Redeemer.[4] This may be a momentary encounter in the college lounge, an expression of praise to God at the ninth hole on the golf course, or in sensing together the majesty of God on the ski slopes. It can be an interlude over the coffee cups at the lunch counter, or a quiet pause in the corner of the living room.

Heretical and impious as this may seem, it appears to be precisely what our

Lord was saying to the woman he met at a well in the province of Samaria.[5] When she suddenly turned "religious" and spoke of their place of worship, He told her that worship is not ever a question of *place.* Since God is essentially spirit, His kingdom is carried about within the believer, to be realized wherever Christians come together to focus on the Eternal. And it is as discreetly dismantled when they separate and go their ways.

Like a Curtain Rising

Christians can choose to make the worship experience a beautifully structured event. They will sense the need to do this, from time to time, but they can also elect to commune with each other in a completely casual way. Whatever the form, they will feel an inner need for worship. It will be something they do, not because they *have* to, but because they want to! Like a curtain rising to reveal a brightly illuminated stage, suddenly alive with people, the Church becomes a living reality when believers come together to worship and praise the great God whose love and joy they have within them.

Whenever the church can be visualized in this way, on the open stage before a skeptical and questing world, I believe that, far from being repellent, it will be magnetically attractive! A hitherto indifferent humanity will scarcely resist the impulse to move forward and mingle with the actors.

This is the image that must have pervaded the first century of the church. It was a ferment so dynamic that the people would risk the terrors of the human torch to get into it. For a lusty Corinthian to be suspended from the believing body, even for an interval of sobering repentance, was a judgment so traumatic as to be avoided at all possible cost.[6] How incredibly the image has changed!

The Happy Kinship

In a sequence of informal visits the hostile Dutchman became a personal friend. I sensed his feeling of alienation. And I tried to help him to see the happy kinship of the Christian and his greater family, the Church.

I can only say he began to listen, and to consider the decision he too would have to make. I wanted him to know that for him, as for many, it was initially *not* a proposition of going or not "going to church," but that the issue was and ever is: What do we know of Christ? Whose Son is He? Has He become our Lord?

When we come to know Him in this way, and begin to gather as His "called out" ones, we find we are reinforced for whatever the day may bring. Here we have a resource that can fill the emptiness that was driving my companion to the other woman's bed. Here is the foundation for peace and harmony in the home. In this relationship we begin to experience the love, the understanding, the security that can send the little Jans merrily skipping off to school!

5

Should we look for it in

A Building, or a Body?

It may be the taxi driver in Rio, or the university student in Tokyo, or a Filipino deckhand on a sea-going freighter—all around the world a person hears the identical question. Why are there *so many* churches?

Whenever I can, I try to explain that things are not what they seem, that in spite of all the appearances that say it isn't so, there is only one church, the Church of Jesus Christ. And that even in this maze of denominations, those individuals who are personally Christian actually belong to the one true Church. For this is true regardless of the particular labels they may happen to wear. As the spiritual sons and daughters of the one Father, the brethren of the one Redeemer, they can and do have fellowship with each other. They have a common bond that ties them together, an allegiance that goes beyond the differing doctrines that would separate them.

Towering Barrier

So there is a way to explain it all, but it leaves me with a feeling of futility. I think of the scriptures affirming that there can be but *one Lord, one faith, one baptism; one God and father of all men.*[7] And I wish to goodness I could tear down the walls, so that people everywhere could see the essential unity, the beautiful simplicity of the one family of God—a family undivided by dogmatics, by race or nationality.

I am not conjuring up some ecumenical Disneyland, based on the lowest common denominator of belief and practice. My sole concern is that people everywhere may come to recognize that there is but one true Church on earth, and that they will muster the courage to live it out as a visible reality.

What has built all these barricades in the first place? Are they there because most of us have either not known what the Bible says, or have never believed it, when it tells us what the Church is? Are we so hypnotized by custom and tradition that we have never thought to look for definition in the New Testament? If so, this is the more amazing because the teaching about the true nature of the Church is at least as clearly laid out in Scripture as the cardinal truth of justification by faith!

Inspired Writers

What can account for the proliferation of churches? I'm convinced the answer lies in the ever-questing, sometimes arrogant, mentality of man. I believe there would be minimal divergence and misunderstanding where people would approach the Scriptures with an unbiased mind, free of a defensive attitude, truly trusting the Holy Spirit to lead them into the truth. What has happened, especially since the Reformation, is that every time some headstrong individualist has hatched a new idea he has gone to the Bible to find supportive material. In a source book as comprehensive as the Scriptures he has been able to pick and choose, and tear out of context, the requisite "proof" for almost any religion a person could conceive.

Apparently it's a question of attitude. Do we approach the Word of God with the anticipation of drawing *from* it, or do we come with preconceived ideas for which we need undergirding and "authority"?

The inspired writers caution us to come with reverence and humility so that from this exhaustless resource we can carry away a rich cargo of truth and inspiration. I am confident that wherever the sons and daughters of God will approach His Word in this way, the resultant unity in faith and understanding will be quite overwhelming.

A Corporate Body

What is the Church? Ask the average Joe, and the first thing that comes into his head is a rather quaint and distinctive building with stained glass windows, and a tower surmounted by a cross. Men of the stature of Paul and Peter sometimes refer to "the church in your house," but they never make the mistake of equating the house and the church. Look anywhere in the New Testament and you will find that the Church is never a building, it is always *people*. The notion that a building can be the Church is quite possibly a reflection of the spiritual sterility that has led church officials to turn to the Old Testament for their concepts of the "house of God."

The Church did not exist in the history of the Hebrews, but the temple in which they worshipped was, of course, a building. It was the place where for a time the Spirit of God elected to reside. But this concept can be imposed on the "new agreement," the New Testament, only by negating the clear teaching of Jesus and the Apostles that the temple, which was initially a magnificent material building, is now the human body, specifically the body of the believer. And, by implication, also a corporate body.

In his first letter to the Church at Corinth the Apostle Paul raised the rather agonized question: *Don't you realize that you yourselves are the temple of God, and that God's spirit lives in you?*[8] (Exactly as God's spirit was formerly ordained to live in the ancient temple of the Hebrews.)

Vibrant Organism

What is the Church? Speak of it again, and the next implication will be that it is an *organization*, massive or small, such as Lutheran, Catholic or Presbyterian. Now if the millions who call themselves by these names were also *Christians*, this would be surprisingly close to the truth, but are they? We can merely say that *some part* of the Church may be found in this or that organization, nor can it be totally identified with any one of the current denominations. This is the more interesting because of the paradox that the true Church *has* organization, in order to function efficiently, without necessarily *being* an organization!

Maybe it's time to blow the whistle on all these illusive conceptions. If the Church is not a building, and is not identical with any existing organization, what on earth is it? The Church is an *organism*, a living vibrant organism brought into being by the Holy Spirit! Like the unlisted phone number that is known only to a few, the number of these millions, disseminated worldwide, is known to God alone. The Spirit of God brings it all together, this wonderful diversity of color and personality who trust in Christ as Savior and Lord.

The Church is the select company of the redeemed. It is that vital and quietly militant minority that is being "called out" of a confused and bewildered humanity to be the salt that keeps it from decay, and to be the light that will focus all eyes on a better world—an eternal world that will transcend the ages of man.

Making It Visible

After individual commitment, the first mile we travel on the road to renewal will be the one that determines our understanding of the Church—what it is, and what it is not, and how it is meant to function.

What is exciting about our time is the evidence that the Lord of the Church is moving to make the whole thing as visible as possible. Some of these demonstrations of Christian community may indeed be faulty, but what is right and commendable is that in these decades in which we live, more and more of the world's people are going to see that while Satan is having his day, God's Kingdom is "alive and well" and *growing* on planet earth!

6

*Has an idea "come to its
time," and is it pointing to*

A New Reformation?

What has happened to the Church is
what happened to Christmas in the engag-
ing story about *The Grinch Who Stole
Christmas.* Perhaps more than anything
else the Church is in need of a kind of
happy rescue that will set it free from the
captivity of the clergy and return it to the
common laity where it belongs.

I do not imply that the clergy has
deliberately entered into a conspiracy to
take possession of the Church, to do col-
lectively what the Grinch accomplished
all by himself (when he stole Christmas
from trusting, innocent boys and girls).
The loss of control by the laity appears almost accidental, as a caprice of early
history.

The astute Emperor Constantine saw the futility of trying to kill off the Christians by persecution as his predecessors had been trying to do. When he found that (despite all that had been done to destroy them) their numbers kept increasing, he apparently decided that "if you can't lick 'em, you join 'em." He made Christian elders the salaried officers of the state, dressed them in distinctive garb, and even appropriated pagan temples and handed them over to the church as elaborate places of worship. Dubious blessings that began the process of regimentation!

A Priesthood of the People

The Reformers reclaimed the forgotten Scriptures about the once thriving "priesthood of believers," but they merely applied them theologically, to show that man needed no intermediary between himself and God. Important as this was and is, it apparently did not occur to them to apply the same truth *practically* to man's ministry to man.

The "horizontal" application may also have been aborted by another caprice of political history—the tragic revolt of the German peasants which had to be suppressed. The provincial princes appealed to the responsible reformers to use the power of the clergy and pulpit to put it down. Lay ministry failed to emerge, at least in part, because of the civic necessity to restore "law and order" to a movement which was widely misunderstood, especially by an oppressed and illiterate laity.

Certainly there was reaction to the segregation of Christians into an "apartheid" of priest and people, but the few faulty attempts to transfer control to the laity were badly handled. Those who tried to practice a priesthood-of-the-people in the aftermath of the revolt were viciously denounced and even exterminated. The focus for change and reform ultimately centered on other doctrines, and not on function.

Incredible Myopia

Generations later, the incredible myopia concerning the need for functional change is exemplified in the experience of a Christian farmer in Norway. Hans Nielsen Hauge, a deeply dedicated man, was denied a freedom of expression he felt to be implicit in Redemption. He was jailed and abused and broken in health because he insisted on telling of his faith in private and public, but without "proper" ordination. Evidence, if we need it, that although the Reformation did introduce a significant quality of doctrinal renewal, *functionally* the church did not change. It has remained under the dominance of the various gradations of clergy, abetted by a strangely submissive laity.

Apart from the negation of Scripture and the apostolic intent, I suppose the clergy-laity arrangement could be defended as a pragmatic way to carry out the commission of Christ, but the truth is that it doesn't work very well. Take a look at almost any "mission church" overseas, at a circumstance where the contradiction frequently shows. We continue to export the clergy-laity pattern to other countries even though it severely limits the normal expansion of the Church. The nationals in these denominational churches quite generally follow the formulas of their foreign teachers, and leave the business of Christian communication to the paid professional.

Functional Change

Eighteen years as a Lutheran clergyman have convinced me that there must be a complete functional change in the way the church attempts to operate. There must emerge a new and courageous spirit that will entrust both the worship and the "work" to the entire body of believers.

This has become so important to me,

personally, that I have relinquished the security of clerical status and returned to the laity. I have done this to identify more fully with the fellow who sits in the pew, and with the others who have left it, but most basically I have done it because it seems to be "right."

I don't recommend this as the immediate route for all clergy. For the man who considers "leaving the ministry" and seeks to establish a new identity, I have a word of caution. It can be traumatic! Even by those who know him very personally he will be regarded as an embarrassing failure, a sort of renegade, a sacred covenant-breaker. At best he will be thought of as a rather confused and unreliable sort of nonperson. He comes to realize that his highly specialized education has left him unequipped for any other profession, and he faces a loss of livelihood until he can reestablish himself in some alternate means of making a living.

Nevertheless it was the step I had to take to be true to an "agonizing reappraisal" of the Church, and to an emerging concept of the ministry that is broader than clerical confines will permit. I am concerned that instead of *helping* the Church, the clergy-laity tradition may actually be destroying it.

Caretaker Ministry

I am aware that by some things I say I will seem to be anticlerical. If we are speaking of the clergy as a professional group, or clergy as individuals, this would not be true. Many of them are my personal friends and Christian brothers. I have strong feelings of sympathy for them and for the dilemma in which they find themselves. But I would have to acknowledge that I am against the clerical *system* because I believe it to be both unscriptural and unworkable.

I would be a callous fool not to recognize, however, that for the foreseeable future there is an important and responsible "caretaker" capacity for clergy to maintain. Most of the Christians are in the denominational churches and will not be leaving. The pew has become a mahogany bastion of security. Many are of an age and outlook that cannot and will not accommodate the kind of change I am talking about.

Legitimate regard, especially for the aging, would indicate how thoughtless it would be to take away their traditional moorings and leave them stranded and bewildered. Generations of pastors and church members have been taught that the existing structure is correct and biblical, and they devoutly believe it.

Peril in Reform?

The very possibility of substantial change would seem to raise at least two questions. Since there *is* peril implicit in functional reform, why talk about it? Why rock the boat? The other is the question of what it would involve. Precisely where would the changes be?

For the source of our confusion about the Church and the clericalized form of ministry, we have to look beyond the political expediencies of a Constantine. We have to turn back to Old Testament Judaism, where only the men of a particular tribe could be priests. These concepts of priest and temple have been liberally borrowed by Roman Catholicism and again appropriated almost lock-stock-and-barrel by unquestioning Protestants.

What we have become accustomed to is not a normal outgrowth of New Testament Christianity. I believe it is rather a narrowing and a professionalizing of a ministry to which every Christian is called. And the free-flowing essence of the Christian life is such that to professionalize it is to kill it. This is what makes functional reform so imperative.

Graphic Metaphors

The Church that is the progeny of the

Holy Spirit is projected in a number of graphic metaphors—the sheep and the shepherd, the vine and the branches, the building stones and the capstone, the body and the head, the bride and the groom. Each describes the interdependent relationship of the believing people and their Lord. For the purpose of understanding the operation of the Church, I think the most helpful of these is the analogy of the Church and a human body, where every organ and cell has an indispensable function to perform.[9]

What it tells us is that, in the Church of our Lord, every member is given a unique enablement and a particular place to fill for the good of all. The Christian community depends on the distinctive ministry of every person in it, to keep it alive and growing. So that this community can function efficiently, the Holy Spirit delineates a minimum pattern of operation. The more mature and responsive are recognized as "elders"; that is, the overseers of each local fellowship or church.

The Original Order

Investigating the original order, we begin to see the radical departures that are the fact of life in the churches today. Let us look again, carefully, at the initial blueprint and consider how it can be recovered and adapted to the urgent renewal needs of our time.

1. The New Testament churches were supervised by a *group ministry*.[10] In the earliest churches these men were usually selected by the Apostles. As the churches grew and matured, the men with leadership ability came to be recognized and were accorded the role of "elder" by a common concensus. These local overseers were normally the older members of the group, both in age and experience. And this multiple eldership explains how it was possible for every member to put in a respectable day of work for his employer, and also participate in an ample ministry in the local church.

2. *The ministers were laymen* who normally remained in whatever trade or profession they followed for a livelihood for themselves and their families. Their ministry to each other and to the world did not depend on specialized education and ordination. In a complete reliance on the Holy Spirit, they found that the same Lord who brought the Church into being also provided for the ongoing life of His body on earth, and that He did this by giving them the entire range of charismatic gifts.

3. The ministry *emerged from among*

the people in the locality. Preachers were not imported from Berkeley or Minneapolis. If they had problems, as they did, at the very least the church was not afflicted with some outsider coming in to assume command and impose contrary ideas.

4. Since the body of Christ is not divided, and does not discriminate in matters of race or gender, I do not see how the every-member-a-minister concept could be denied to women and applied only to men.[11] The one exception to this would be some of the leadership roles for which the Word of God has generally indicated men.

Second only to the confusion about the essential nature of the Church, the biggest roadblock to renewal is the misunderstanding of the ministry. And of all the challenges we could bring to "the Wittenberg door" none will be more difficult to realize. Yet I believe the change to a church-of-the-laity will come, not through prestigious councils and commissions, but as a folk movement of ordinary men and women who trust in the order and control of the Holy Spirit. And who see the recovery of the New Testament pattern as the only plausible way to carry out the unrevoked mandate of our Lord, to communicate the Good News to our neighbor wherever he is, and wherever we happen to be.

7

Doctor, do you have

A Prescription for Recovery?

When Dr. Helmut Thielicke's book *The Trouble With the Church* came on the market some years ago, I bought it and began to read it with considerable interest. For the symptoms of the "sickness" that prompted Thielicke to turn his pen into a probing scalpel are more and more unmistakable. In large sections of Thielicke's Germany only one or two percent of the membership appear for worship services. If as many as eight or ten percent of the people surface on a Sunday morning, in any part of Europe, the bishops are all but skipping and dancing in the aisles.

Because fairly large numbers "go to church" in America, we have the illusion of good organizational health. But I believe the decline that has long since come to Europe will be just as apparent on this side of the Atlantic by the end of the decade. It will show in the empty pews and the vacant pulpits.

Wistful Optimism

Some of the more conservative seminaries can still point to rather substantial enrollments, and their presidents voice a wistful optimism about the future of organized religion. But the occasional production peaks on the seminary charts do not give us an adequate perspective. The various denominations across the country show more valleys than peaks. Finding that a survey of eleven seminaries showed an average enrollment of less than a hundred, one national Board of Theological Education let the axe fall on over half of them.

In Latin America the seminary situation in practically all the major denominations is nothing less than desperate. To cite just one example, an impressive campus in Buenos Aires, built and stocked with books, beds, and classrooms to accommodate three hundred students, currently has twelve. There is considerable shaking of heads and wringing of hands but little or nothing in viable alternatives to meet the massive decline that the seminary crisis would predict.

Getting back to Thielicke, I can only say

that I was disappointed at the superficiality of what he had to suggest. I thought surely his diagnosis would isolate and come to terms with the prevalent emphasis on "sacramentalism." I was amused as he rather cleverly skewered the current craze for liturgy, and pleased that he offered no new trapeze numbers for the ecumenical circus.

Gratified that a person of such prominence would move to admit the symptoms of sickness, and let down by his diagnosis, I was even more amazed at his prescription —more and better preaching in the churches! To me it seemed incredible that a man of his intelligence and perception would not recognize that his remedy has been rendered inviolate purely by precedence and human tradition. If the learned doctor of theology would take another look at the derivative wordings in the New Testament, he would see that he was repeating a prescription that will only aggravate the sickness.

Words for Preaching

Without going into scholarly semantics we need only point out that there are six Greek words which the Bible uses to describe the act of preaching. Let's begin with *laleo* which means no more than making oneself heard. Then there is *diaggello* which means "announce"; *katagello* which means "advertise," and *dialegomai* which is rather poorly translated "argue" and better expresses as "enter into dialogue," which was Paul's favorite way of opening his communication with non-Christians.

The other two original terms are *kerusso* which means to "herald," and *evangelizo* which means, of course, to evangelize or tell good news. With the possible exception of *laleo,* which indicates no particular audience, did you notice the direction of all these terms? That they are unmistakably saying that "to preach" is to make the message known to the people *outside* of the Christian community?

To announce, to advertise, to herald or proclaim, to tell good news, can only mean one thing—the New Testament writers clearly intended that what we call preaching is not to be done in the church! The dynamic announcement of the Christian message is to be directed to the world of humanity beyond the confines of the Christian fellowship. This may be done through the mass media and in the public stadium, but these descriptive words also include the kind of impartation that is most effective in a person-to-person encounter.

News, good or bad, can only be news to those who have never heard it. It is no longer "news" to people who have listened to it a hundred times. Whatever the quality, stimulating or mediocre, liberal or evangelical, I believe the churches are sick and dying precisely because they are being preached to death!

Instrument of Rescue

Now the question, if the approach to the gathered Church is not to be preaching, then what? I can think of no better place to take our cue than from the first assemblings of the Church that was born at Pentecost. The writer says *they devoted themselves to the apostles' teaching and to the fellowship, to the breaking of bread and to prayer.*[12] Not one word about preaching!

The life-giving glucose that can bring healing and growth to the body of the believer, individually and corporately, is the teaching of the Word of God. The instrument of rescue and resuscitation of the person without hope is the preaching of the Good News.

Corrective Option

If it matters to us that the churches are declining and dying, we have a corrective option here—to reconsider the place of preaching! When we ignore the counsel of the inspired writers and do as we have done for more than a century, reversing the direction the Gospel is ordained to go, the effect is lethal in place of life-restoring. To sit and listen to preaching Sunday after Sunday, even to evangelical preaching, may not produce the growth of spiritual life. It can, instead, harden and callous and destroy.

After a quality of preaching that leads to awakening and conversion, the critical need is to get the patient into the "recovery room," into an atmosphere that will call forth the gifts of the Spirit from among the members of the newly gathered body of Christ. Some will respond to this in a way that will indicate how the Holy Spirit is moving—to provide for the instruction that the body will always need. Others in this body will discover they have been given the particular capacity to tell the story to the "waiting world."

8

Is there anything
sacrilegious about

An Informal Approach to
the Almighty?

Responding to a rather desperate long-distance call from a pastor who was leaving for a convention without a Sunday replacement, I thought to myself—can it be possible that there isn't a single one of these two-hundred-plus church members who can be trusted to say anything intelligible about the Bible or his own experience? But there was no time for musing or questioning. The fellow with the urgent request was a personal friend, and I subsequently found myself before the mysteriously forbidding altar and behind the once-familiar pulpit.

Prior to the worship hour I had a chance to renew my acquaintance with several who had been with me in a series of conversational studies on the Christian faith three years previous. By the close of our time together some of them were breaking through to a clear and exciting articulation of their life with God. It dismayed me to discover that in the brief interim they had not progressed, but had actually retrogressed, in their capacity to express anything at all about a personal spiritual life.

Had there been no new insights? Had nothing been happening, so there was nothing to talk about? I believe I found a piece of the puzzle in the carefully controlled liturgical service that followed.

Truth Becomes Cliche

Certainly there are some positive things that can be said about liturgical worship. Coming in from a world of disorder, disquiet, pollution, social pressure, financial anxiety—preoccupations in which we have been very much involved, we can sympathize with the natural wish to spend an undemanding "oasis hour" away from the hubbub and as totally detached as possible. The need for this is accentuated now that the home is so rarely a quiet refuge for the hurried and the harried. It is more typically a Grand Central Station of comings and goings than a place of rest and restoration.

We reason that we have been giving of ourselves and now we have come to receive. Having hired the best available specialist to provide us with inspiration and uplift, we feel we have a right to collect on our investment. For church members that do not read the Bible (and that's a sizable crowd) here is a chance to hear it read and explained. The weekly repeating of group confessions and ancient creeds will eventually root, in the subconscious, at least some of the elementary doctrines of the Christian religion.

But the same repetition also robs them of dynamic and personal impact. It offers little or no stimulus to conscious or creative thinking. When truth becomes cliche it can lead to indifference!

Some of the prescribed prayers are quaint and devoid of contemporary content. Other prayers in the book are masterpieces of poetic completeness. To some degree it may be helpful to go along with the liturgist, to try to enter into these prayers and let them express what we might wish to say. But the more they go beyond our normal speech and thought patterns, the more these flowery phrasings will diminish and cripple the prayer life of the person in the pew. Once given the inference that, to be valid and respectable, prayer must be eloquently shaped and sculptured, what ordinary novice is going to open his mouth to pray in public or even in private?

Stifled Talent

In the strictly liturgical production where any spontaneity is considered a rude intrusion, even the choice of the hymns is preempted from the people who have come to worship. Travelling around the country I have listened to more complaints about this than any other item in the Sunday bulletin.

I have also been exasperated at the lack of imagination on the part of missionaries who have assumed the superiority of our European-American heritage of hymns and liturgies, and have introduced them into foreign settings where they frequently fit very badly. Often they are poorly translated and crudely combined with the musical scores. What is most disturbing is the stifling of native talent and creativity which must inevitably result from a forced mutation of this kind. Surely these nationals are being cheated out of their spiritual birthright.

Communal Desire

In many churches the potentially enriching experience of the Lord's Supper is vitiated by an assembly line ritual that makes it a hurried and meaningless formality. The dear ladies who have to put themselves on display at the communion rail can be forgiven if they are more conscious of their skirts and nylons than of anything the sacred meal is meant to convey! I wonder where we got the idea that this is to be done on a stage, in full view of the audience, rather than in the center of a small worshipping circle?

What prohibits any such freedom of movement is another anachronism of a bygone age, the omnipresent pew. I have a growing suspicion that this monastic device is the devil's ultimate invention—gleefully calculated to make worship impersonal and fellowship impossible! The very architecture considered appropriate for the liturgical setting militates against the natural participation of the laity. The vaulted arches, intended to inspire awe and reverence, have the concomitant effect of muting and intimidating. A rather high price to pay, surely, for all this contrived dignity when a structure of substantially less cost and opulence can be far more functional.

Liturgy, per se, is not an evil. It merely represents the communal desire to approach the Almighty in an orderly and meaningful manner. The question is, whose order? Ours, by voluntary selection and creation? Or an officially authorized "order," imposed by some upper-level hierarchy? Apparently there has always been an overpowering "mustn't ever touch" complex about liturgical tradition. The notion has persisted that to be valid and respectable it must be as Shakespearean as possible!

I suppose we can be encouraged by the current trend toward liturgical innovation. Some of the contemporary "folk masses" are spirited and pleasant, with particular appeal to youth. No matter how much horror the orthodox have felt toward those who dare to tinker, the latterly concern with updating the liturgy does demonstrate at least one positive thing—that liturgy has always evolved. It has not fallen as golden printing plates from heaven. It merely expresses the changing worship requirements of generations of people.

Festival of Praise

Would it not follow that, to be appropriate, liturgy must also be indigenous—rising out of the worship needs and aspirations of the varied national cultures? I doubt that it can be imported or exported without the risk of violence to the other heritage. As liturgy manifestly has evolved in the past, it must be given the latitude to grow and formulate again, out of the corporate experience of the worshipping laity and according to the needs of the "now" generation.

Rethinking the place and the purpose of the liturgy is one of the areas where sensitive minds will "cross a border." Writing to the Christians at Ephesus, Paul insists that the secret of a good life is to *be filled with the Spirit.* In expressing this life they will *speak to one another with psalms, hymns and spiritual songs.* And he tells them *to sing and make music in your heart to the Lord, always giving thanks to God the Father, for everything, in the name of our Lord Jesus Christ.*[13]

In an almost identical paragraph he tells the body of Christ at Colosse to *let the word of Christ dwell in you richly as you teach and counsel one another with all wisdom, and as you sing psalms, hymns and spiritual songs with gratitude in your hearts to God.*[14]

In both of these localities he seems to suggest the beautiful simplicity of informal worship. Those who gather to worship God will always have the need to innovate and avoid stagnation. And this is where a stimulating sequence of songs, of Scripture and response can make a contribution.

These gatherings can be unstructured and casual, but they will lose nothing of the unction of the Spirit where there is also prior planning. A pattern I would like to see actualized would find the Lord's people dispersed into small groups for informal worship for about three consecutive weeks. Once a month these groups would congregate in some suitable public building to celebrate their intrinsic solidarity in a well-planned festival of praise and prayer.

9

Are we forgetting to provide

A Place for the Children?

To see a son or a daughter turn away and begin to leave the church out of their lives—this is a major heartbreak of many a mother and dad. Especially for those who have taken them there as toddlers and well into their teens. Having tried to set the best possible example, they wonder where they have failed.

We who may want to communicate our Christian faith have frequently had the next encounter with these sons and daughters at the other desk in the office, and as a neighbor across the fence. And we generally find they rebuff any attempt to interest them again.

Some of these will, of course, do what custom requires. They will have their babies christened or baptized. They will possibly make an effort to get the children to Sunday school. If there is a marriage in the family it will certainly be a "church wedding." They will attend a Christmas program and an Easter service. But what they will demonstrate, supremely, is that for them the church has no meaning.

What has created such an image of displeasure or distaste? Where did it all begin? I remember a well-dressed couple marching their seven children to a front pew, every Sunday without fail. And there they sat—in a stiff, tailored row, like so may bright and colorful manequins! Watching the weekly tableau, I had the disquieting sense of being an unprotesting witness to a subtle form of cruelty.

Mistaken Counsel

"Church" can be a time of acute discomfort for the alert child. Hushed into monastic silence, he finds he is trapped and immobilized by an interminable sermon projected at the parents who tower around him. He may be conscious of insufferable tedium and the desperate wish to get out of there, go to the restroom, any possible exit from the ordeal at hand. Is it any wonder that he *does* escape it all when he gets old enough to make his own choices?

A long succession of preachers have been telling us that we are to bring our children to church. This is to be the measure of our piety and responsibility. And this is why it will be difficult to begin to appraise the issue from another perspective. What has been so generally applauded as exemplary and proper may have been very mistaken counsel!

If we are searching for factors in the wholesale abandoning of Christianity by the youth of a church-going tradition, we may very well begin by assessing the impact of repeatedly taking children into an environment where they have had to endure the indignity of being ignored, with needs unmet and unrecognized. In the loss of our youth we may be harvesting what we have so carefully sown.

Identical Need

I would question that any person, under teenage, should be compelled to sit and suffer through an adult service of worship. Subjecting a child to a performance directed over his head, and forcing him to conform to adult standards of response, can inculcate an utter dislike for any such situation. And as the process lengthens into years the feeling of aversion is very effectively reinforced. When he eventually removes himself from all that has tormented him, is he not merely doing what he has been thoroughly conditioned to do?

If adults have the need to be met at their level of interest and comprehension, isn't it fairly obvious that children have the identical need? And wouldn't a recognition of this be essential in worship as well as in Christian instruction? As we consider the alternatives, let us look first at the Sunday school hour that customarily precedes the service of worship.

After an "opening exercise" which may be skillfully handled and pleasant, or quite innocuous, the child is received by the well-intentioned lady who has accepted the task of teaching his class. More than likely she is a volunteer teacher and is totally untrained. She may or may not have any aptitude for the job. Whatever the prescribed lesson contains, she will primarily convey her own vague moralizations about religious life.

If it is inexpensive babysitting we are after, this may be a flawless solution. In all other respects it may be a complete disaster! It frequently means that our Janes and Johnnys are exposed to a meaningless theology that bears no relationship to the life they are living. Very commonly they will walk away from the class with conclusions contrary to what the teacher intended.

Clear Correlation

It may be helpful to recall that "Sunday school" was originally conceived of as a means of "mission" outreach. The idea was to offer at least a minimal Bible knowledge to the kids "across the tracks." It was directed to the children of families entirely out of touch with the church.

Children of Christian parents were to be taught at home. The renowned reformer and teacher, Martin Luther, would have been aghast to see this responsibility delegated to outsiders. He prepared his unique and popular catechism to help such parents to get the basic outlines of a truly Christian viewpoint and to pass this on to their children. There is undoubtedly a correlation between the biblical illiteracy of this generation and the abandoning of the practice of teaching children at home.

Somewhere along the line (and it's a fairly recent innovation) the churches began to lose the fervor of Sunday school outreach and expropriated the entire program for internal consumption. Rechanneled to serve as a curriculum for the instruction of the children of church families, the "church school" has become a very inadequate option.

We who would like to recover the vitality of New Testament life will need to

consider the quality of Christian environment that can produce it, and which will
equip "the company of the committed"
with something valid to share with their
offspring. Positing this kind of reinforce-
ment, the job will not be as overpowering
as it seems. The major reason that parents in general know so little, and are so
utterly unqualified for the role of instructor, is that their sole exposure is to a
form of church life that has left them un-
challenged. Fundamental to even a rudi-
mentary grasp of Christian belief will be
what the parent learns through participation in the weekly experience of communal
teaching and worship.

Forum for Learning

Those parents who feel they need more
orientation than this, and what their individual study of the Bible provides, could
band together for more systematic instruction—which is to say that if there is going
to be a "Sunday school," let it be for the
schooling of the parents!

The home is the natural setting for the
constant, casual teaching of Christian
values. It will take time, perhaps the cur-
tailment of some of our fraternization, but
the project is worthy of the best that we
can give. Even a daily mealtime can be
an open forum for the bantering about of

much that is important.

Some of the richest times we have had with our own family have taken place when we backed our chairs away from the supper table, and our children have shared a verse of scripture that had real meaning for them. The insights they have gained in ordinary living have often blessed and inspired us all. Gradually becoming aware of the place of the home in providing Christian instruction, we have tried to follow the Lord's command to the people of Israel: *You shall therefore impress these words of mine on your heart and on your soul. . . . And you shall teach them to your sons, talking of them when you sit in your house and when you walk along the road and when you lie down and when you rise up.* [15]

Wide Horizons

Perhaps an evening a week, or on a Sunday morning, the family would find it essential to sit down together to study and discuss a biblical guideline somewhat more deliberately. And they might prefer to do this in the company of another family or two. Here are wide horizons for Christian creativity!

Beyond the responsibility retained by the individual family, when the believers gather for worship as a community, the children can join them in an opening period of praise, prayer and song. Then those under teenage may preferably be taken aside in the care of two or three adult couples who will minister to them in a lively worship experience of their own. A plan that works well in a Christian community in California is to rotate this parental requirement each month. As with any movement, the Church of our Lord needs to recognize that what it will give to other generations will depend on how meaningful it is to the children.

10

What can we learn from

The Farland String Band?

As a boy of twelve I was sort of lend-leased to an uncle, to help him hand-milk his eighteen cows. Returning home a year later, I heard my mother talking about a "string band." I remember the intimation of pride and pleasure whenever she spoke of it. Something new and strangely alive had stolen in to brighten the dull "depression days" in our prairie community. For at least an evening a week she could forget the grinding poverty, the unpaid taxes, the empty granaries.

A string band? I wondered what on earth it would be like, but all I got was a happy chuckle when I pressed her to tell me more.

"You'll see. They're coming to our house."

And then they came. A fellow in his early twenties carried a violin. His teenage brother had a guitar. Three from a neighboring farm brought another violin, and one had taught himself to play the mandolin. Someone strummed an autoharp. Two sisters and a friend over the north hill joined in the singing. A young girl from the town livened up the atmosphere with her witty, bubbly personality.

Throbbing Vibrance

There was a little self-conscious banter as they began tuning their instruments, one bending to hear the other strike a chord. Some were undoubtedly a little off-key, but when they launched into a gospel song I was entranced, breathless, ecstatic! Here was a vibrance, a throbbing aliveness I had never felt before. Their tunes had the bouncy rhythm and swingy sound of "country western," but to me they excelled all the symphonies we had listened to on our Atwater Kent radio.

Hard-working dads in faded overalls and moms with rough gnarled hands relaxed in the corners of the room, for the string band was indeed a "family." Proud and pleased, occasionally whispering a comment to a neighbor, they listened, and how they enjoyed it! It was good to know that their youngsters would not be spending their time in the boozy bowling alleys and pool halls of the town.

Springtime of Youth

The lines of a song still linger with me from that first awestruck evening:

"Jeg har fundet en frelser sa yndig,
Mit i ungdommen's sjoneste var . . ."

It came from their hearts, with real joy shining in their eyes, for the words are a witness to personal faith. "I have found a wonderful Savior, in the beautiful springtime of youth."

When the band began to slow down, and some were pausing to uncramp their fingers and rest their voices, the ladies of the house brought in cocoa, coffee, doughnuts—and a lively social interval. At the close, the eldest in the group (the one whose dream it all had been) got up and read from the New Testament. After a comment or two he prayed, and others prayed, simply, naturally, in their own words. Some of their elders joined in, praying in Norwegian. All blended their voices in the Lord's Prayer and then it was over. Someone invited them all to his home the following week.

My one obsession after that night was to get old enough, and to be able to sing or play "good enough" to get into the string band. I also found they shared a positive conspiracy—they wanted you to be a Christian "so you could sing to the glory of God." They had taken a motto from one of the Psalms: *Sing forth the honor of his name: make his praise glorious.*

I was searching, not too sure of my relationship with God, but in time they let me in, apparently confident that such as I might "catch" the Spirit from the rest of them. Actually there were no exclusions. If you had an instrument you took it along and played it. If you had none you came and sang. If you couldn't "carry a tune" you did your best.

In our community there was a brief "summer school" for the teaching of religion, but our Scandinavian parents had no tradition of Sunday school, so there was none. There was also no youth organization, nor was there any need of one—the string band eventually attracted and absorbed practically all of the young people in our country church. The band met every requirement for Christian socialization. In the winter we had sleigh rides and tobogganing in the hills. In the summer we had picnics and evening campfires.

Positive Impact

Taking our cue from the stagecoach stop from which our township got its name, we called ourselves the Farland String Band. Occasionally we were invited to sing in other churches. We took a few brief tours beyond the neighborhood, but the band never did aspire to be polished or professional. It was enough to be together, to sing for enjoyment and "for the glory of God." It is a measure of the impact of this corporate experience that these young people have literally scattered to all parts of the country, as pastors, missionaries, teachers and leaders in local churches.

The young "folk movement" that so wonderfully ministered to the needs of my community was not occurring in the churches around us. They struggled to maintain the customary young people's leagues and organizations, with the usual see-saw sequence of failure and success. Devout parents agonized over their indifferent offspring and did their best to involve them in the church, but it was often a defeated effort.

What can we learn from the Farland String Band? I suspect that where youth programs fail it will be found that the adult planning is usually premised on highly spiritual objectives, desirable to adults, without actually considering what might be appealing to the youth. Materials are prepared and policies are established with a commendable purpose "to win and to hold our youth for Christ."

We set up all kinds of meetings. The young folks are given official titles, and organized around a core of religious content—Bible studies, role plays, discussion topics, and the like. And we wonder why they don't beat down the doors to get in!

Fish are not interested in the fisherman, only in what is on the hook bobbing in the water. We tend to forget this when we focus on youth and try to attract them into the Kingdom. And we may quite radically modify our thinking before we begin to succeed. If we take teenage motivations into account, we will very possibly settle on some activity other than a religious one!

Larger Family

Christianity has acquired such an indelible image of dullness that it is no longer enough to announce a "meeting." It seems that the day has passed when it would suffice to call our young people to another church gathering, so why not consider a complementary attraction? And oddly enough the song group has come full circle, and is again quite up to date.

We are gratified by the turned-on Christian minority who choose to center on solid study of the Bible, but this may not be the point of initial challenge for the many who are mentally or bodily "outside." In a small church the choice will be narrowed down to basically one activity, but in the larger churches there can be a wide and exciting diversity—depending on the locale, plus the skills and talents available among the adults. If not a "core program" of music, how about a ski group, a back-packing group, a company of car rebuilders or a sailing armada?

Looking at Jesus in His boyhood, Luke says He grew *both in body and in wisdom, gaining favor with God and men.*[16] Whatever the activity, I believe the focus should be on building—physically, socially, intellectually, spiritually—with the ultimate goal of helping a boy or girl to find a secure and satisfying place in the larger family of God. In a very substantial sense this puts the burden of success or failure on the "models" who live out the life of Jesus in their total existence. For the colorful and attractive lures that arrest the attention of the young must metamorphose, in time, into a love and admiration of the fisherman, too, and for his Lord!

11

Can we encourage

A Grandstand Religion?

I never was a Beatle fan, but I'll admit they did more than kick off a whiskery, hairy rock band craze that swept over the world like a williwaw. They had the droll audacity to stand up to the Bernsteins and the Ormandys, to walk into places like Carnegie Hall—to demonstrate that the half-literate street boys of Liverpool can be wonderfully creative, with or without credentials. They dispelled all doubt that such as they can stir and disturb and stimulate, even if what they do is a you-name-it, and some of us have a hard time calling it "music." They can gather in tenements and pool rooms and beat out exotic sounds to captivate the human spirit.

And it isn't only the sound—sometimes raucous, dissonant, unbearable; sometimes haunting and beautiful. The Dylans and the Beatles, and those who followed them, have jarred us awake and made us aware of the gloom and despondency of a generation without faith and hope. They (and the ubiquitous folk singer) have often slapped us in the face with a message we would otherwise never have heard. These roving, restless bands of today's balladeers have something to say to our fat and complacent society, even if it comes as a cry of despair. They fling it out to the wide world in the versatile caparison of song.

Uninhibited Creation

It isn't surprising that the Christian youngster, too, would catch the rock band fever. Leaving the pew sitter to labor through the quaint hymn tunes of a dead yesterday, the new breed of believer moves on to explore and innovate. He recaptures the lusty courage of a young Luther who took even the tavern songs and made them shout the good news of redemption. And he doesn't only borrow and recast the old nostalgic melodies. He dares to unleash the hounds of uninhibited creation. These Michaelangelos of Song tell the universe of youth and age that Jesus lives, that His Kingdom is here, and here is life!

I could go on and rhapsodize; there is

much that I admire and applaud. Yet there are implications that raise a caution or two when this carnival of sonic syncopation is highlined into a Christian setting. All is positive and commendable if it is not manipulated to package and commercialize the Christian faith (just as the rock world has done, to push and proliferate their philosophy of drugs and death). When this begins to happen in either of the two kingdoms, whether of Satan or of God, I believe that the alert Christian will cross a barely definable border.

Happy Diversion

It's great in the basement and living room, this Spirit-inspired beat of bass and drum. It's fine on the platform of the local church and school. As a happy diversion to lift and entertain the home folks in the locality, good and well. As a way to bring the gang together and tootle away the evening, splendid! But it can be perverted when we put it on the grandstand and send these kids across the country to advertise religion.

However titilating it may be to the churchy audience, the subtle impact on the one employed as a purveyor of religious belief may be something less constructive. The repetitious parroting of ever so excellent Christian testimony can depreciate and "monotonize" an initially exciting conviction into tedious platitudes.

Some few may have the maturity, the inner stability, the spiritual stamina to counter the creeping erosion of a very personal faith. But young people are sometimes pressed into situations where they are professing, in public, far more than they have experienced in private, and much more than they are living out in their daily existence. I have seen these accomplished young performers come back from the tour, abandon their Christian cohorts and cash in on the night club circuit. I am not at all sure that evangelical promotion should take its cue from the Beatle brand of commercialized performance.

Are we not warned against following the ways of "the world"? *Everything that belongs to the world,* says John the Evangelist—*what the sinful self desires, what people see and want, and everything in this world that people are so proud of—none of this comes from the Father; it all comes from the world.*[17]

Spectacular Evangelism

What goes for the group with the new sound and song goes for the Big Show genre of spectacular evangelism. And it goes for all the Big Daddies who have made made it so colossally as to catch the eye of president and potentate.

In all fairness, there is undoubtedly a sizable number who date the beginning of renewed hope and purpose from one climactic night in the public stadium. And for this we can be glad and grateful. But for every person added to the Kingdom, by such methodology, isn't it quite possible that other hundreds are subtracted? Distracted, too, from the modest every-Christian-a-communicator intent of the Stephens and Phillips and Pauls who set the pace, showed the direction, and laid out the original pattern.

What may appear so unquestionably good and irreproachable can have a fallout that is bad. When the big dramatics are over, Joe and Jane may go home with the very mistaken impression that if we mean business about evangelism we will make it a huge and expensive spectacle. They will also carry in their consciousness the debilitating heresy that the effective evangelist is invariably an expert, a professional, a polished artisan of the trade.

Something More Audacious

It is impressive, and it surely seems audacious, to watch the Big Man who stands before the hundred-voice choir and moves among the bright lights to hurl the message across the arena. But isn't it much more audacious to stand alone in a crowded classroom, to speak a trembling word in response to the hostile attack of the academics? To counter, by your silence, the ribald remark in the locker room? To reach out to the other carpenter on the scaffold with a touch of love and sympathy for one who has lost a son in a car crash?

It isn't easy to detach yourself from the crowds that follow the Pied Pipers of our time, but I believe these are the appropriate settings for a communication of personal faith. Valid alternatives to grandstand religion.

There is, of course, a laudable place for Christian entertainment, and for the talented and Spirit-impelled entertainer. Christian audiences may, in fact, have a greater lack of quality diversion available than their non-Christian neighbors, for the simple reason that there are fewer acceptable, "Saturday night" options open to them.

The point I would make is merely that the Christian performer who elects to go beyond the basement and living room, to enter the public arena, should in all integrity call the tune what it legitimately is. What is clearly and unashamedly labeled *entertainment* will not then be confused with some dubious form of "evangelism."

12

Is there a priority for

A Witness Without Words?

I would like to return, for one brief interval, to a favorite theme—a conviction that in the initial approach to the world around us, practically all effective communication of the Christian message is nonverbal. Unless I totally misunderstand him, this is what the Apostle Paul is affirming for the Church at Corinth when he says: *The unspiritual man simply cannot accept the matters which the Spirit deals with— they just don't make sense to him for, after all, you must be spiritual to see spiritual things.*[18]

Countless years of dedicated missionary endeavor and millions of dollars have been dissipated by the failure to grasp the implications of this basic insight. One who seemed to understand it was Toyohiko Kagawa of Japan.

Toyohiko was born of the illicit union of a Geisha girl and a wealthy Kobe merchant. Orphaned when he was four years old, and shunted from place to place by uncaring relatives, he missed the tender touch of a mother's affection and the security of belonging. Then, as a lonely boy of sixteen, he discovered the love of God in the warm acceptance of a foreign family. And he was overwhelmed. He decided to give all of his life to the sharing of this kind of love with as many as possible of his fellow Japanese.

Meeting Human Misery

When he had completed his college and theological studies, he went back to his home city and settled in the slums of Shinkawa. There he met poverty and human misery beyond anything he had ever imagined. He chose to live as most of the people lived, in a three-tatami room (six by nine feet). He earned his daily bowl of noodle soup by sweeping chimneys in the industrial district. He shared his hut with homeless beggars and his rice ration with hungry prostitutes.

Finding that the slum laborers were cruelly exploited by the factory owners, he encouraged them to group together. Then he would go with them to voice their grievances. They were met by gangs of goons employed by the factory bosses, beaten bloody and sometimes senseless. Toyohiko spent months and years in ratty jails, but his efforts began to pay off in a better life for the people of Shinkawa. In time they began to be curious about his motives. They began to come and ask, "Why do you do this, Toyohiko?" "What are you hiding from us?"

And to everyone who asked he would tell of Jesus and His love. He told them of the carpenter's Son who walked along the roads of Galilee without a place to call His own. This man named Jesus who shared His bread with drunkards and harlots, who touched the eyes of the blind and made them see. This Jesus who always had time to listen to the troubles of the tax collector that everyone hated.

Toyohiko was a myopic old man when I met him. Long ago he had shared his bed with a beggar who gave him the trachoma that left him nearly blind. He wasn't very impressive to look at, and now he is dead. But there are thousands of Japanese who have followed Jesus because they first met Him in Toyohiko.

Demonstrated Love

Nearly blind as he was, Toyohiko saw

clearly what so many have never understood. That the non-Christian can only comprehend the message of Christ as he *sees* it in an obvious and practical demonstration of love and concern, a love that reaches out to touch him at his point of need.

Many who are the recipients will never respond with gratitude of any kind, but there will always be those who will wonder and there will be some who ask. And then we can tell them, in words, what we have been telling them by what we are doing. We find there are those who have been awakened out of their indifference, mysteriously "turned on" by the Holy Spirit. Now they can respond to the spoken message of redemption.

In a parable of the final judgment, Jesus tells of the Son of Man who will come in splendor and take His seat in majesty.

All the nations will be assembled before him and he will separate men from each other like a shepherd separating sheep from goats. He will place the sheep on his right and the goats on his left.

Then the King will say to those on his right: "Come, you who have won my Father's blessing! Take your inheritance— the Kingdom reserved for you since the foundation of the world! For I was hungry and you gave me food. I was thirsty and you gave me drink. I was lonely and you made me welcome. I was naked and you clothed me. I was ill and you came and looked after me. I was in prison and you came to see me there."

Then the true men will answer him: "Lord, when did we see you hungry and give you food? When did we see you thirsty and give you something to drink? When did we see you lonely and make you welcome, or see you naked and clothe you, or see you ill or in prison and go to see you?"

And the King shall reply, "I assure you that whatever you did for the humblest of my brothers you did for me!" [19]

What is He saying here? I believe He is telling us that the world is tired of words and sermons. That people everywhere are waiting for the touch of human compassion. They are looking for the person who will not see them as disembodied "souls," or as potential statistics to impress the ecclesiastical hierarchy. They are looking for the Christian emissary who will see them as people, and who will give of himself and his means to help them where they hurt.

Practical Incarnation

When they sense our concern for their poverty, or their loneliness and alienation, they may be moved to respond to the wonderful words of the Christian gospel. What is required of us, who make up the body of Christ in the world of today, is that we first begin to demonstrate the love and the peace we talk so much about.

Have we thought we were to preach to crowds of strangers? To irritate our neighbors by banging on their doors? To build ornate boxes on the corners of their towns? We had good intentions, but we may have been wrong!

We have come to a new horizon, and the Lord of life is beckoning us to cross over. He is asking us again to consider what *incarnation* means. To learn, at last, that the Word must first become flesh—warm, human flesh and compassionate spirit.

Isn't this the way we first met God? We saw Him in the One who became a human being and lived among us. Then we began to grasp the wonder of His truth and the beauty of His grace.

We are called to take His place. To live as He lived, to give our life as He gave His. To reenact the incarnation for those around us.

13

In spite of all that has happened,
Can We Be Brothers?

Once upon a time it must have been clear that if you wanted to interest an Indian in the Christian faith, you saddled your horse and rode out to the lodging where he lived. You sat where he sat, you ate what he ate, you warmed yourself at his fire. He made you sensitive to his hopes and dreams, his problems and preoccupations, and you let him know they were valid. You did your best to affirm and support him in his greatest concerns. You did whatever you could, by the giving of yourself, and you did it in a way that would not rob him of esteem.

When he wondered what you wanted for yourself, you assured him you had no other motive than the love of God—lived out in very human personality. You convinced

him that believing in your Lord he could
have a superior life, a felicitous blending
of the native and the redemptive. He found
peace in the new understanding of the Great
Spirit. He began to recommend the reborn
vitality to his family and people. Many followed his lead, and together they began
to worship the God they met in you and
in your Book.

The new communion of native country
men was uniquely their own. They endowed
it with a distinctive genius that flowed from
generations of tribal custom. They origi-
nated songs and chants, prayers and ways
of worship. You were welcome to sit with
them in their circles, to break bread, to
share an experience or a teaching. You
were their brother, but when you came
among them you came as a guest. You accorded them the confidence they merited
and did not impose your patterns.

A Dream Demolished

Ah, but it is only a dream—a dream
shattered in the dust before the door of a
hundred thousand hovels, cold and bare,
with broken windowpanes. A dream demolished by the lack of discerning love,
and by heady intoxication with simplistic
philosophies about "the American melting
pot." The personal, the private, the individual and tribal is supplanted, now, by a

mistaken image of democracy—issuing in a sodden, oppressive conformity. Anything outside of it is suddenly suspect and subversive, oddly out of step. The laboratory beakers are all poured into one mammoth bottle, to be shaken into one splendid homogeneity!

And there is no need, now, to go out and look for Mohammed, for Mohammed has come to Mecca! The Hebrew has settled in Manhatten and the Arab is in Chicago. The Negro has migrated to Harlem, the Puerto Rican to Brooklyn. The Indian has moved to Minneapolis, the Cuban to Miami, the Mexican to Los Angeles, the Chinese to San Francisco and the Japanese to Honolulu.

Nevertheless these exotic denizens are not to seek security in their own racial affinities. They are not to segregate, but to integrate, even if it means the transporting of little children across the exhausting city. We are to compel them to democratize!

Yet we don't let them buy the house next door because that could lower our real estate. And we certainly don't want them to marry our daughters, for that would mean miscegenation!

Faded Flowers

The seasons come and go, and we wonder why no flowers bloom. Why the crowded inner cities burn and smolder. Why all optimism has withered in the wind. Why these "colored folks" don't appreciate us. Why they refuse our invitations. Why the churches are still white, and a pitiful few are black, or tan or bronze.

My Anglo-Saxon confederate, how short is your memory and mine! How quickly we have forgotten the character of our immediate past. Our grandparents came from Norway and Finland, Germany, Italy and Holland. Didn't they live in sheltered communities, and worship in their ethnic churches? Didn't we, like them, speak our native idiom and sing our traditional songs for several generations? Until we dared to mingle, until we were ready to live and worship with other cultures and share the general vernacular.

We needed "reaction time," even we with a common Caucasian heritage. We who had not seen our families decimated by the invader's diseases, or murdered by callous marauders, grasping for land and gold. We who had never been driven from our hills and forests and prairies, and herded into barren reservations. We who had never been hunted, chained and carried in reeking ships across the sea. We who had never been bought and sold.

Passive to Militant

Am I angered and defensive when the

black man calls me a honkey, and the Mexican a yankee? Am I vindictive and irritated when they prefer the society of their own people? When they band together under the slogans of Black Moslems or the various Indian movements? Am I indignant when I read of young Indians who risk their lives to preserve the fishing rights our treaties "guaranteed" them?

Ground into the degrading dirt of poverty, despair and civic indifference—isn't it conceivable that they have to do these things? That they also must go their own way for a while? That my darker-hued compatriot *has* to learn to say and believe that "black is beautiful" and "red is respectable," or whatever? That he has to be able to live with himself before he can live with me?

If we have deceived ourselves into assuming that the options are all ours and, because there are more of us, he is to be compelled to come to our side, to integrate with us in our overpowering society, I believe *we* have a border to cross, an alternative to ponder. Surely the Lord must be saying again, as He said to the man who had killed his brother, *The voice of your brother's blood is crying to me from the ground.*[20]

If we who claim to be Christian would win the love and loyalty we have lost, then surely we must go to him—in the humble spirit of our Lord. And must we not allow for him, as we did for ourselves, the crucial years of adjustment and reaction? Yes, and even more, stand by him in the painful interval of conflict?

Overwhelming but Possible

We are called to acquaint our countryman with our Lord and with our Book of Life, but when the introduction has been made I believe we must step back and let him discover the body of Christ among his own. When he is ready, he can choose to invite us in or leave us out. But the option has to be his.

What seems overwhelming to man is ever possible with God. Impelled by the Spirit of Christ and gradually merged into one, I believe we can be brothers again.

14

Are there particular hazards for

The Man in the Collar?

When Jim Patten walked into a Kenmore tavern and sat down to talk with a stranger, he had no inkling of the tempest he would set in motion. It has blown over, now, but the problem he brought into focus lives on. The issue is relevant because it is unresolved.

If Patten had been a carpenter or a bank manager, there would have been no problem. But Jim was not an ordinary tradesman; he entered the tavern as a seminarian, and hence a fairly typical representative of a prestigious church body. The stranger he had been talking to turned out to be a man of the press, who was intrigued with the novel idea of using a tavern as a hunting ground for "mother church." The thing was especially titilating because of

Patten's attempt to interest the "go-go" girls performing there.

Appropriate Rage

When the news of Jim's rather original missionary approach hit the headlines, his superiors reacted in appropriate rage and indignation. Jim was called on the carpet, and the tangy affair was catapulted all the way to the archbishop. When Jim would neither apologize nor repent, nor curb his operations at the tavern, he was confronted with discipline and dismissal. His fellow seminarians threatened to boycott their classes if such a thing should be carried out. They defended the option to do his own thing.

We can sympathize with the dilemma of the archbishop and his equally strong conviction that a seminarian could not be allowed to bring reproach on the Holy Church. The irony is that both the aroused seminarians and the boxed-in archbishop were right. And they were also wrong!

As a Christian, and as a plain citizen, Jim Patten would normally have complete liberty to go anywhere, even to the bars and taverns—if these were the haunts he opted for, to be in contact with the world as it is, and to offer help and counsel to people as they are.

People in crisis, people with crushing

problems, are not generally seeking help in the churches. They are going to taverns and the night clubs. What should inhibit a concerned Christian from electing for these places as a personal parish, determining to offer the hope and the resource we have uniquely in Christ our Lord?

Beat for Christian Outreach

The churches have rarely considered the counsel of the Apostle John that the Christian is to be "in the world," while maintaining an identity with Christ and His church that can keep him from being assimilated, and also becoming "of the world." [21] No doubt the Jim Pattens of our day are seeing that the super abundance of meetings and masses and membership drives have created a ghetto existence that insulates their ministry from the real world where people are. So Jim could be right in choosing the workingman's tavern as his particular beat for Christian outreach. But the archbishop would be equally right in insisting that he was mistaken in his choice.

Why the contradiction? Because Jim did not go there as a typical citizen. He went as a holy man, a priest, representing what is assumed to be the repository of all that is holy and proper. Inadvertently he was spotlighting the barrier to communication that a professional religious role automatically creates.

Every now and then the media will feature some flamboyant preacher who gets the grudging attention of the public by hitting the night spots, but he is obviously out of his element. I don't believe a priest or preacher can pull this off without raising the suspicion that he is double-timing or otherwise compromising "the ministry."

Confined Image

I certainly do not condone these suspicions. I merely emphasize that they are there, whether we approve them or not. They are there because of the peculiarly confined image of life and ministry the churches have projected. It's an utterly unreal and mistaken image. I believe it is in total conflict with the intent of the New Testament. But because it is there, in the mind of the agnostic and Christian alike, it can hardly be ignored.

It is understandable that the clergy occasionally rebel at this, and attempt to crash the barrier by going out with the boys to "hang one on," or conspicuously downing cocktails at a party. I will not soon forget the shock and revulsion pervading the entire coach when a reeling, wise-cracking chaplain staggered aboard a commuter train filled with sailors returning to the base after a night of carousing in San Francisco.

Clergy simply can't have it both ways, and they might as well recognize it. The rite of ordination sets them apart and imposes a "curfew" they have to accept and observe. Those who habituate in Sodom run the risk of soiling their cassocks and confusing the image of the One they represent.

Free to Minister

The Christian laity, in stark contrast, is free to minister anywhere, without these hazards of stigma or reproach. So if we are concerned with potential arenas for the sharing of liberating life, we are pressed again to consider our calling. The issue is not whether Jim Patten had a right to do what he did, or of the archbishop's action to denounce it. The question is whether a believer (Patten, Connally, Johnson or McDougal) should ever be cast in a role that can so drastically curtail his activity.

15

Is there no other way to be involved?

No Script for the Layman?

Alf Nelson worked with his uncle in a furniture store in Seattle. The pay was not astronomical, but he liked the job and he looked forward to becoming a partner in the business. Then the draft board began "breathing down his neck." Since he could not, in conscience, get involved in killing, he had to scramble for alternatives to going into the army.

Alf also felt a strong attraction to the Christian ministry. He was typical of a core of dedicated young fellows who would gladly go on any errand, to help with the work in the rapidly growing church he attended. Under pressure also to try to get draft exemption, he spoke to the pastor about his urgent sense of "call" and was approved by the church board as a lay assistant.

For Alf the immediate consequences of his decision were good. He would not be blinded, killed, or maimed, nor face the loss of irreplaceable years in any ill-advised military escapade in some remote corner of the world. But there were other consequences that were less affirmative. Quitting his job at the furniture store meant the drop-out of one more young and winsome personality from the ministry of the marketplace.

And at the church it meant the loss of opportunity for a number of Nelson's colleagues! If there was a youth gathering to be led and directed, Alf was there to do it. When there was need of a substitute speaker or Bible teacher, Alf was on salary to do these things. The fact that he did them ably and well could hardly compensate for the diminished incentives for others, perhaps less able and experienced but equally willing to serve, on a voluntary basis.

Tomiko San

The coming of the missionary family to the industrial town of Kariya, Japan, created no great stir among the clapboarded shanties where they settled. In time they got acquainted with several of the young wives and mothers whose husbands worked in the factories. These friendly and curious ladies were eager to learn about American customs, and began to drop in for a cup of tea. With many an apology for their assumed inadequacies, they offered to help the missionaries in any limited way whatever.

Their willingness opened the door to some basic instruction in the Christian faith, and enlisting their help in passing it on to the children of the neighborhood. This led to the formation of a bustling little "Sunday school" entirely managed by some of these talented women who thoroughly enjoyed the new outlet for their creative energies.

Then came Tomiko San, fresh from the Bible school in Shizuoka, to be employed as the "parish worker" in Kariya. Viewing the highly original and sometimes unorthodox mission to the children with quiet distaste, she set about to "correct" what they were doing so as to conform with the models she had learned about in Bible school. It did not help that she was an outsider and spoke a different dialect.

The result of the implied criticism was a general feeling of disappointment, a nursing of wounded sensibilities, and a gradual disenchantment. One by one, the ladies began to withdraw and return to their former ways of living, before the missionary and the church had come to their town. The withdrawal of the mothers meant the absence of their children, and within a year the promising beginnings in Kariya came to an end. The presence of a "professional" was more than the ladies could cope with.

Carlos

Carlos was not just making a casual visit to the parsonage in the Brazilian city where I was the parish pastor. I could sense that there was something bothering him, and after the customary greetings he came right to the point: "Our former pastor used to keep after me to go to the seminary, to prepare for the ministry . . ."

His honest, ruddy face mirrored his feeling of puzzlement and reproach. Why hadn't I been pushing him in the same direction? Certainly he had the usual qualifications. He was active in the church and was doing an exceptional job of leading the Sunday school worship service. He was a trusted employee in a local bank, working conscientiously to provide for his wife and two children.

I said, "Yes, Carlos, I'm sure we could arrange for you to go to the seminary at Porto Alegre but, if you leave, who will take your place? Who, then, will be our Lord's ambassador to the Bank of Minas Gerais? Isn't it just possible that Christ called you to be His minister there?"

Carlos was probably the only Christian

in this large and prestigious bank. I also knew that whenever there was a discrepancy in the accounts, showing that one of the clerks had pocketed someone else's "cruzeiros," the manager invariably turned to Carlos for help in tracing the missing funds. He had earned a reputation for integrity, even the grudging admiration of his loose-fingered colleagues.

A Larger Perspective

Carlos was both surprised and intrigued by what I had faced him with. He suddenly realized that his job offered opportunities for Christian ministry that he had never considered. And he was relieved to know that he would not have to upset his wife by moving away from the home community and separating from parents and relatives. He could continue at his work without compromising his inner "call" to be faithful to his Lord.

Carlos went back to his job with a larger perspective, an awareness that it was something more than the manipulating of money and a way to get his groceries. He began to think of it as a personal precinct, his point of contact with the many around him who clearly needed a fuller dimension of living, a goal and a purpose beyond the temporal.

Carlos was also involved with several

of our leading laymen in a topical study of Redemption and of avenues to Christian growth, and shared in a ministry of outreach to neighboring villages. There was gratifying evidence of spiritual response. Some were beginning to *be concerned above everything else with (God's) Kingdom and with what he requires.*[22]

I felt the work was progressing well when the executive committee of the Brazil mission came up with a plan to recruit the outstanding men of our congregations for a mini-course at the seminary, after which they would be sent out as "full-time" lay ministers. Inevitably Carlos, too, was caught up in the excitement of what appeared to be a much greater vision than mine.

Along with a select number of others who were beginning to move up in the business world, he quit his job and enrolled for a cram course in preaching and theology at Porto Alegre. It seemed not to matter that this meant a general uprooting of these men and their families when they were subsequently dispatched to other cities and towns to work in the churches.

Ultimate Question

What happened to Carlos (and to Alf and Tomiko) has been occurring through a hundred years of mission history. Talented men and women have been removed from their normal occupations and pressed into positions that could only prevent the emergence of a truly indigenous church. What has been termed "lay work" is rather a professionalized parody of legitimate local ministry.

Men such as Carlos have been victimized by these ill-conceived programs, divorced from their normal occupational contacts, and made to live out their lives in uncongenial circumstances. Zealous propogators of the church at home and abroad have displayed an incredible insensitivity to the evidence that to professionalize lay activity is, to a large extent, to neutralize and to limit the normal ministry of the laity.

Such "professionalizing" is not necessarily effected through specialized education. Although it does entail the risk of setting some apart from others, where it does not require the severing of community ties and family relationships, instruction in a Bible school can be highly contributive to local ministry. What we need to recognize is the particular impact on those who can be enticed away from their natural vocations, and placed on the payrolls of contrived and traditional church operations.

What can overcome the inertia of the worldwide Christian mission? I believe the one great hope of a turn-about lies in a radical return to the New Testament standards of life, worship, and outreach. There is ultimately only one question: Can we or can we not trust the Holy Spirit to produce this vibrant life for us, to lead us into all essential truth, and to give us the gifts and enablements that will mean an effective and satisfying ministry for every believer?

16

Why can't there be a "full-time"

Call To Be a Carpenter?

A star basketball player embraces Christian faith and begins to consider how he can invest his life and abilities in the service of Christ and His Kingdom. He talks to his Christian friends, he listens to sermons on commitment, and seeks the counsel of the college chaplain. And he rather quickly gains the impression that there is only one way to be an all-out Christian, that unconditional dedication points in one invariable direction. If he is to give first place to the Kingdom of God, he must enter "full-time" service and become an ordained minister. And, if he is to do the ultimate, he will go the final step and become a "foreign missionary."

The young impressionable athlete is given to understand that it would be selfish and "secular" to follow his natural inclinations to become a high school coach. It would be something other than putting Christ first in his life. Instead of going on to a legitimate career in mind and body-building sports, he is diverted into the traditional channel of clergy oriented "service." He pulls himself away from the exhilarating sound of the referree's whistle, the pulsating whirl of the hoops and hardwood, and spends his ensuing years in a struggle to master the intricacies of ancient Greek and Hebrew, and braving the terrors of pulpit homiletics.

Lacking the disposition for highly constricted relations with parish-type people, and a natural bent for public communication, he lives out his life with the disquieting sense that he may have been misplaced. He is troubled by nagging doubts that he can ever accomplish what is required of him. He and his family, and not least his parishioners, suffer the pains and frustrations of his struggle to conform to a role for which he is clearly unsuited.

Brief Interlude

An attractive young secretary volunteers to enter "full-time" service as a missionary. Although her dedication would be unquestioned, her decision is nevertheless complicated by a particular coincidence.

She is also on the rebound from a disappointment in love when she feels the "call"
to leave the country and go to a "mission
field."

After a brief interlude of language study
she finds herself alone in a strange village,
trying to adjust to the baffling culture patterns of an unfamiliar society. She quickly
senses her ineffectiveness in the unac-
customed missionary role and attempts to
compensate by "going native," adopting
the national modes of dress and diet.

Less than a year of rice and seaweed
malnutrition, of debilitating loneliness, of
constant inner frustration, a total feeling
of inadequacy—and all these things begin
to take their toll. We find her jetting home-
ward, in the care of a companion, with a
nervous breakdown from which it takes
long years to recover.

Recurring Denominator

What do the lady and the athlete have
in common? The recurring denominator
is confusion about "the call" to Christian
vocation. This is further complicated by the
clergy-laity disparity which implies a dis-
tinction between "full-time" and "part-
time" Christian commitment. And it fosters
a sacred-secular segregation in the minds
of church people. This feeling of division
has been intensified by a seemingly inno-

cent device, such as the Service Flag!

The "flag" had its origins in the wake of World War II. When a son of the congregation entered military service, his pastor and family proudly added a star to the "service flag," reminding the people to pray for his care and safety. As the war continued, there were the sobering occasions when a blue star was replaced with a gold one, signifying that the final "taps" had been sounded for one who gave all he could give for his country.

After the war ended it occurred to someone to convert the Service Flag into a promotional gimmick for Christian activity. When a son or daughter in the church left for seminary or mission work, a blue cross was added to a Christian Service Flag.

Again it had a commendable purpose. It was to be a reminder to pray for the one who had volunteered for "full-time" Christian employment. What no one thought of, apparently, was the implication that, by the same symbol, every other Christian in the congregation would be relegated to secondary status!

Factor of Confusion

A more significant factor of confusion that we need to take another look at is the concept of "the call" to Christian service. Since I was unsure of my own "call," even after entering the seminary, I made it a point to confront every pastor, missionary and evangelist who came across my path and ask him to define his "call." I got some oddly contradictory answers, and I generally noted a feeling of irritation and defensiveness.

Several claimed to have heard an audible voice, others told of dreams in the night. Some told of particular circumstances that made their individual call unmistakable. Conspicuous, by its complete absence, was any sense of universality in the comprehension of this call!

Not Merely to Dream

The problem was finally resolved, for me, through the reading of a book by Oswald Chambers. This devout Englishman, with a touch of the mystic, had a capacity to explain the operation of the Holy Spirit with remarkable clarity. In the book entitled *So Send I You,* he develops an analogy in which he compares the call of God to "the call of the mountains" and "the call of the sea."

Out on the western plains where I grew up, my brothers and I loved to scramble to the top of every hill and scoria-capped butte for miles around. In that section of the country there were no mountains to challenge us, but I have since come to know men and women for whom climbing mountains is a life-long passion.

Up there in the treacherous heights, in a total spending of strength and stamina, the dedicated climber seems to undergo a subtle transformation. There are days of danger and flirting with death. There is intimate acquaintance with peril and privation, and the exhilaration of conquest. Through it all, something of the elemental nature of the mountains gets into his blood and into the core of his being.

Now he can no longer look at a towering crest without the awareness of a strange contagion, a very personal sense of "call" to scale and conquer yet another mountain. The "nature" of the mountains within him responds to the mysterious attraction of the mountain heights. His inner spirit is attuned to the "call" of the mountains. It is a call not merely to dream but to act, and he will be restless until he returns to the towering haunts were he is most intensely alive.

Chambers had found that the call of God is like that. Essentially indefinable, it comes uniquely to the one in whom God's own nature has been formed. It is like the irresistible call of the alpinist in whom the very nature of the mountains has become an integral element.

Chambers went on to say that the call

of God is like "the call of the sea," and with this I could identify more fully because for several years I had followed the sea. First as an ordinary apprentice, standing watches and swabbing the decks. Then as an Able Seaman, manning the booms and winches. And finally as a Mate on the bridge, charting courses and taking my turn at command.

Living with Danger

The seaman, too, learns to live with death and danger, loneliness and privation, rampaging storms and shipwreck. But in countless days and nights, in months and years of intimate communion with the open sky and sea, something of the essence of it all becomes a part of him. He may deceive himself into believing that the life that matters is the life ashore, but a few days of the scurry and scramble in a teeming port city compel him to return to the unhurried solitude of the sea.

He finds himself pacing the waterfront, he hears the long blast of the whistle, signaling that a vessel has completed her cargo and is ready to pull in the gang plank. He listens to the pounding of the winches hauling in the lines, and suddenly he feels the familiar inward "pull"; he hears the "call." And in a matter of days he will be out there again, where the gulls fly and the swells rise and fall. It is nature calling to nature, the spirit within responding to the spirit of the open sea.

Spirit Responding to Spirit

These metaphors of mountain and sea help to clarify what the call of God is like in the life of a believer. For if we were to try to define the essence of the Christian's faith, we would have to say that what has happened is that something of the infinite nature of God has become a part of him. And now there is a starting point for communication.

Nature identifies with nature, spirit responds to Spirit. God, the Redeemer, continually calls to his own implanted life within the heart of the believer. He beckons, he speaks, he "calls," to everyone who has received His Spirit. No one is omitted. *You are a chosen people, a royal priesthood, a holy nation, a people belonging to God, that you may declare the praises of him who called you out of darkness into his wonderful light.*[23]

I would question the general notion that there is an exclusive call to clergy and missionary. It comes to every Christian, to every man and woman who has been willing to receive into his or her inner being the life and the Spirit of Christ! He calls each one of us to put His Kingdom first, and to serve Him by our concern for the neighbor and brother. It is a call to unconditional commitment of all of our time, talent, and potential.

If I sense no such call to follow and serve my Lord, it can only mean one of two things —either I have not understood what this call is, or I have never experienced the rebirth of life and purpose that His Holy Spirit brings.

God's Engineering

Where we may go and what we will do, in response to this universal "call" to ministry, is a matter of God's "engineering" of our every circumstance. Some will be led to serve the Lord in other countries. Others will be directed into equally essential ministry in the homeland. If we look for His leading, He will always accommodate to our level of understanding.

When God's call is viewed from this perspective, our pulpit becomes the place where we work and our parish the place where we live. Our normal contacts—as a mechanic, a carpenter, a banker, a teacher, a housewife or a secretary—constitute the "field" into which we are called and enabled to serve our Lord, and to share in the building of His Kingdom.

It becomes crucial to discover the career

which our abilities and limitations will indicate. An adequate concept of Christian vocation takes away the artificial distinctions between the secular and the sacred. It opens the entire spectrum of legitimate occupations as a basis of selection. It conceives of work as a potential source of pleasure, and as a kind of therapy that can enable us to enjoy life in its fullest dimension.

17

Must there be a pause

At the Seminary Gates?

Stretching for a bit of humor on the all-too-somber occasion of a spring commencement, theological deans will sometimes play on the alliteration of "seminary" and "cemetery." I wish we could smile and let it pass, but it isn't a joke—I am convinced that seminaries *are* the cemeteries of the Church!

The deep desperation of the philosopher Nietzsche still rings in our ears. "What are the churches, if not the tombs and sepulchers of God?"

Before his rejection and scorn of the Christian faith he had evidently gone to the churches in a search for truth and, finding it obscured by ritual and tradition, he assumed it was not there! One can only wonder how different his philosophy may have been if he could have looked in on a simple gathering of God's people as they were in the beginning.

It isn't only the liberal and secularized seminaries that are busily digging the graveyards of the Church. I believe that any institution, established to systematize the Christian faith and to professionalize the Christian ministry, may very possibly become the pallbearer of that faith and ministry.

Process of Suffocation

Admittedly there are certain fundamental beliefs that Christians hold in common. The question is, can this basic body of faith be boxed and packaged without suffocating it? For the process of suffocation occurs in the conservative and orthodox schools of theology as well as in the free-wheeling liberal ones. The worthy intent of the biblically oriented theologian is to distil and unify Christian truth, yet the tomes he may produce frequently become the spawning ground for further division.

The endeavor to clarify and isolate the distinctive elements of the Christian faith, in the manner of a C. S. Lewis, can be entirely commendable as long as the resultant theology is not imposed on others as a mandatory creed. (Apparently it is then it becomes divisive.) And of course we have much to learn from Augustine, Luther, Calvin and their spiritual offspring.

Nevertheless the dynamic nature of the Christian religion is such that no theological system will be conclusive. The infinite wisdom of God cannot be compressed into any adequate formula.[24] There is always at least one piece of divine intelligence that defies labeling and categorizing into our neat and finite theologies. Hence the lesson of history is that sooner or later the seminary "cafeteria" will likely have one of two offerings on the menu—a rather militant liberalism or a dead and static orthodoxy. And either entre means ptomaine in the bloodstream of the Church.

Radical Diversion Point

Aristocratic Englishmen of a century ago had a hobby of searching for the headwaters of the Nile. If we are to seek out the precise point at which the concept of the Church is dammed up and continually diverted into institutional channels, I believe the quest will take us directly to the seminary gates. It is the radical diversion point at which the Church ceases to be a movement of the laity and becomes the docile prisoner of a clergy-dominated complex.

The disorientation which the seminary experience may foster is discernible both in the professor and the pupil. A primary peril the teacher of theology faces, especially as the curriculum has become highly specialized, is the incipient boredom of repeating and perpetuating a certain set of concepts and ideas. In quiet desperation he frequently begins to innovate. The "death of God" philosophy that so fascinated the news media some years ago is quite possibly only one example in a long roster of innovations that have had their birth in boredom. Other instructors begin to ride their private hobby horses and become specialists in ecumenics, glossolalia, liturgics, tame or violent social revolution.

When we focus on the student, we can see that his exposure to seminary disciplines may infect him and disorient him in several areas of his conscious thinking.

1. *In personal faith.* Christian belief, in many seminaries, is disected and intellectualized to a degree that is largely destructive and self-defeating. We send our men to these institutions so they will get to know the Bible and will maintain the purity of our doctrines, but the end result is frequently the precise negation of this intent. Many come back to the churches with the unsettling sense that the Bible is unreliable, and they incline toward a playing

down of the experiential in the life that a knowledge of Scripture is meant to produce.

2. *In communication.* Seminaries tend to become rather unique towers of babel, incubating a brand of jargon that only the seminary-oriented can understand. Christian concepts are codified into a rather bewildering diversity of philosophical semantics that the average layman neither can nor cares to comprehend.

3. *In geographical dispersal.* Seminaries have almost invariably had the effect of uprooting men from the native locality and a periodic transplanting in alien soil. Implicit in such dislocation is the basic misconception of Christian vocation we have previously spoken of, and the failure to grasp the essential geographic unity of the Church in any given locality.

The Parishioner

The detrimental impact of traditional theological training, on professor and pupil, has also led to a disorientation of the parishioner. A constant packaging of religious experience into a kind of perpetual theater, where one is invariably the actor and all others are spectators, does not produce the mutual ministry that the Church must recover in order to survive. Perhaps our "mid-week Bible studies," the "small group movement" and the "living room dialogue" endeavors are actually a subconscious cry for liberation, an admission that we may not be doing the right thing on Sunday!

Christians are having to relearn the custom of coming together into the particular groupings where growth in articulation is possible. There is a need to reconstitute a more total "family" environment in which they can come to know their potential and begin to share it with others. And they frequently find that for every shared insight and experience there is someone in the group with a corresponding need. Can a valid ministry evolve in any other way?

Wherever believers gather and place themselves under the pervasive influence of the Holy Spirit, there is an actualization of the authentic spiritual climate in which the individual believer becomes aware of the distinctive "charisma" which the Spirit dispenses. Such charismatic enablement is not reserved for some specially trained caste of religious Brahmins, to be forever set apart from all other untouchables. The true charisma is for every believer to communicate, within and beyond the community of the redeemed. And it does not divide and confuse. It *unites* in love, humility and understanding.

Rich Diversity

The various listings in the letters of Paul merely indicate the rich diversity of enablements given to meet the needs of the growing churches of his time. The attempt to confine these enablements to any exclusive enumeration may not be productive. Allowing that some of the basic needs remain constant, the requirements of the Church of today may certainly differ in some particulars. Can the concept of the charismatic be limited to a "nine gift" cluster, given such definitive billing by some of the Pentecosals? The grace-gift, or "charisma," covers a far wider spectrum as applied to the Christian community by the New Testament writers.

In essence, what the apostles are saying to every generation is that the Lord of the Church stands ready to give precisely those abilities that will keep it alive and growing—both internally, within the life of the community, and externally, for a penetration of society that will at last extend to every creature on earth.

And I believe we should let these God-given abilities be expressed and recognized in the language of today. I question that we are meant to imitate the precise phraseology of a church that operated hundreds of years ago in Corinth.

A Sense of Delight

How can these gifts be consciously realized in the life of the Church? Through a sense of delight and ready responsiveness, some will become aware that they have the charisma for teaching—a gift intended primarily for the immediate needs of the community of believers. In the frequent expressing of a steadily growing faith, others will gradually come to know they have the gift of communication to the outside world. Many will be happy to discern that they have the distinctive empathy and the healing hand of the shepherd. They will be enabled to stand by their brothers in the hour of crisis and discouragement as the true pastors of a viable Christian society.

When it is not hampered by division or neutralized by irrelevant organization, the Church will provide what it requires—a richly faceted ministry of men and women who love and follow their Lord and express, in all "horizontal" relations, the peace and the joy the Spirit produces.

In summary, and in contrast to the artificial clergy-laity segregation which seminaries have fostered, let us again consider the ministry from the apostolic perspective.[25] In the blueprint that Jesus and the apostles have left us, essential ministry is to emerge from *within* the Christian community. It is to be a *group ministry* of mature men and women who do not abandon their individual occupations. It is to grow and evolve out of the worship and fellowship experience, as they assimilate the teaching of Scripture and the learning of the local gathering.

Where there is a need of intensive instruction, beyond the immediate potential of a local gathering, it can be provided by gifted men and women who are called of the Lord to itinerate among the churches. These instructors can offer a basic curricula and share their teaching in occasional seminars.

Recovery of Principles

I had not noticed, until recently, a significant part of Paul's defense before Agrippa. *So then, King Agrippa, I was not disobedient to the vision from heaven. First to those in Damascus, then to those in Jerusalem and in all Judea, and to the Gentiles also, I preached that they should repent and return to God. . .*[26] (Acts 26: 19, 20, NIV).

Paul began where his new life began. New Testament ministry is to find its initiation in the home vicinity. It is to move in ever-widening dimensions into the larger community, the city, the state, the nation and the world. In a recovery of the principles of post-Pentecost life, I believe seminaries will be superseded by an understanding of the Church that will render them unnecessary. I firmly believe that when the Christian community is given the liberty to function in direct dependence on the Holy Spirit, it will produce its own ministry. It will do it as naturally as the trees around Wenatchee, Washington, produce delicious apples.

* * *

I'm thinking, here, of theological institutions as they currently exist. It would perhaps be rash to say that a seminary could not serve in some other form or context. But I would question that the existing structures could so reform and restaff as to meet the needs of the new day in the emerging community of Christian laity. More than likely the altered situation will require a cessation of what is now, a breaking of the mold, an entirely new beginning.

Can the relevant instructor be a product of the current clergy-laity pattern? Will he not necessarily be a person so firmly rooted in lay community that he will be able to teach from this perspective, and from this frame of reference?

18

Does the Bible give us

A Blueprint for Lay Worship?

Isaac Stein had been a "Jew for Jesus" long before it became a slogan. I met him in the high open shed behind the office of the Stein Lumber Company. He sat down on a slingload of two-by-fours and relit his pipe. I said I had been doing a little thinking about the worship of the early church. I wondered if they might have gotten some of their ideas from the synagogue, and I had a couple of questions. I knew Old Isaac loved to reminisce about his Hebrew heritage. As always, he was ready with a literate answer.

Stein: "There undoubtedly was some kind of a 'carry over,' maybe unconsciously."

Stenberg: "Like having elders in charge of the congregation?"

Stein: "Right. We had them in our synagogues. But more significantly, the Christians who came out of Judaism likely carried away a sort of 'conditioning' from the character of the synagogue itself."

Stenberg: "The character of the synagogue?"

Stein: "Yes. From its inception the synagogue was called 'the child of the dispersion.' This refers to the scattering of the Jews after the fall of Jerusalem. When the temple was demolished, the synagogue began to flourish. That's when it came into its own as a radical departure from earlier places of worship."

Stenberg: "Radical? How so?"

Stein: "To my people it was most certainly radical. The synagogue didn't have to be in a holy place like Jerusalem; it could be anywhere. It had no sacrificial or sacramental ritual. It did not require a special priesthood."

Stenberg: "That sounds like a lay movement! Did this mean that any colony of Jews could start a synagogue?"

Stein: "Precisely. Then, as now, a group of Jews might establish a synagogue and share the responsibility for the conduct of its affairs. You see, the synagogue is essentially democratic. It represents a fellowship of worshipers seeking God through prayer and study."

Stenberg: "Not too different from what Christians did for a couple hundred years! Would there be other similarities, for instance in liturgy?"

Stein: "Yes. In the common use of the Psalms in worship, both spoken and chanted. In the public reading of scripture, so arranged as to expose the worshiper to the entire Word of God. And, even in temple times, there were the small gatherings of the devout for the study of the sacred books."

Stenberg: "Thanks for your help. And now I won't take any more of your time."

Graphic Symbols

The New Testament Scriptures appear to be almost purposely reticent about the *form* by which a particular practice is to be carried out. Baptism, for instance, is commanded, but no mandatory mode is indicated. The sacrament of the holy communion is instituted by the Lord himself, the essential elements are given, and frequent observance is clearly implied, but again there is no invariable procedure which is required of His followers. Believers have noted certain scriptural examples, and the connotations of the graphic verbal symbols relating to these sacraments, and have developed a diversity of application within these broadly unifying doctrines.

Again, when they speak of the worship of God, the New Testament writers do not lay down definitive formulas. They seem to assume that God's people are to be led of the Spirit into an enriching variety of worship experiences. Perhaps the door is deliberately left open to the distinctive expressions of the Christian faith that would flow from the varied nationalities and cultures that would embrace it!

Discernible Elements

It is not surprising, then, that in the reference to the vibrant worship life which sustained the people of the Pentecost event, only four elements are mentioned. Luke says, "They met constantly to hear the apostles teach, to share the common life, to break bread, and to pray" (Acts 2:42, NEB).

Let's take a look at each of these components and consider what they tell us about worship.

1. *Teaching.* Those who had been awakened, and turned to follow the Redeemer, had an urgent need to get an understanding of all that lay before them. A nation of people whose every breath and action had been circumscribed by laws, rituals, priests and temples, now find themselves facing the awesome liberation of the New Covenant. It must have been something

like the feeling of a London artisan who, having abandoned the secure and predictable society of Old Europe, one day stands among the towering firs at the end of the Oregon Trail!

Believers are still grasping for the guidance and direction that can give them a foothold in the strange and marvelous new frontier of faith. Those of us whom God seems to have called to be the "trail guides" into an authentic community of Kingdom people very soon confront the enormity of the mental transition that these people are faced with.

At first it will seem deceptively simple. Just call a meeting and cite the elementary principles that the apostles laid before the Spirit-born assembly! A few of the disenchanted from the old establishment will eagerly attend. But the irony is that they will not realize the extent to which they have been conditioned by their former associations with traditional Christianity. And they will come with deeply entrenched expectations to have the need for the refueling of their faith provided for them, *by others* in the group!

The leadership will sometimes encounter the super-pious notion that the Holy Spirit can operate only in anarchy. For some who have been accustomed to a carefully monitored "order of service," the pendulum will swing to an extreme that will permit no order at all! These may be of the conviction that to be "spiritual," a worship gathering must offer a jolly miscellany of random choruses, "popcorn prayers" and ejaculations. I suppose we are all one part Corinthian!

This mentality fails to realize the necessity of at least a minimal "order" and progression. And a need for easily discernible *transitions* which can enable the participant to focus and refocus on each successive aspect, as the corporate body moves from one part of the worship to another.

Apparently worship requires a differing flow of mental and spiritual energy for each distinctive element. Singing, for instances, is easily entered into. Sharing and teaching demand more concentration, and prayer—a rather total identity of being. Where no leadership is exerted, and no cues are given, it can generate in unease and a tension that makes individual empathy difficult, and participation all but impossible.

So the content of the teaching must bear heavily on the biblical references that define what the Church actually is, and the essential role of the initiator and the elders. The record is there, in the Acts of the Apostles and the letters they wrote in times of crisis, and for clarification and encouragement. These concepts have to be carefully ferreted out, pondered and prayed over. I'm convinced that much of this foundational teaching must *precede* any serious attempt of a questing nucleous to enter into a communal type of worship. It can't be hurried or detoured. I have learned to appreciate the careful preparation David and Karen Mains did before they launched the Circle Church experiment in Chicago. They took two years to chart the course and lay the groundwork with a cohesive core of determined "pioneers."

2. *Sharing the common life.* One could fervently wish that this little statement —expressed in other versions as "fellowship" or "brotherhood"—had been amplified to. tell us all it may have involved! No doubt it describes the general "feeling of family" the first Christians enjoyed, both in their casual and communal relationships. Yet "sharing" and "fellowship" can scarcely be thought of apart from spoken utterance. Quite likely there was general participation, particularly in the smaller gatherings.

3. *Breaking bread.* This can of course have reference to their custom of sharing the available food and eating their meals together. Yet we need not ignore the devoted line of Bible commentators who

have understood these words to speak in the context of worship. In love and obedience, and as an integral part of their worship of God, the early believers bowed their heads and gratefully shared in the Supper of the Lord.

4. *Prayer.* I don't suppose there is any question of sequence that would place this part of their life together, last. Prayer pervaded the very atmosphere when "the followers of the way" joined hearts in worship. It would be unproductive to speculate whether these words of prayer were spoken before, during, or at the close of the worship interval. We remember the instances where they prayed prior to an event, as in the selection of an apostle. We find them praying during a crisis, the night when Peter had been arrested. At another time they raised their voices in praise to God after Peter and John were released and returned to them by the prison officials. Prayer must have been the "vital breath" in all phases of their worship environment.

Sunnyside Fellowship

My son and I happened to be along in a rather spontaneous experience of worship that began with a small counter-culture group in western Washington. Because the house where we met was located in that suburb of Everett, and simply because they needed a "handle," they came to be called the Sunnyside Fellowship.

Without attempting to follow them in any particular order, we kept before us the four principles of worship from Acts 2:42. Through the first fall and winter we met on Sunday morning, but eventually we found that more would participate if we met in the evenings. These gatherings around the Word of God fell quite naturally into a sequence of four parts.

1. *A time of socialization*, in a potluck supper brought together without any particular planning. Some of our number were unemployed, others were students with little income. The potluck enabled those of us who "had" to share with those who "had not." It helped us to get to know the new arrivals, and it gave us a chance to romp with the children in the group.

2. *A time of singing* helped to create an atmosphere of joy and adoration of the Lord that brought everyone together. It enabled us to sort of "shift gears" and gravitate smoothly into a spirit of worship. It also acquainted us with the current Christian folk tunes, and we learned to appreciate those of a more enduring quality. In this part of our worship, gifted individuals felt free to introduce original songs.

3. *A time of sharing* focused on grate-

fulness to God for guidance and other blessings. As the group matured they shared "lows" as well as "highs." And we began to recognize that sharing insights "from the Word" gave more substance to our worship than simply the sharing of subjective experience. The former seemed to move us toward worship, while the latter related most naturally to fellowship.

4. *A time of praying* was often prefaced with the reminder to think primarily of those things for which we could sincerely praise God. Generally this time of prayer, which closed our meeting, also included requests for particular needs. The prayers were brief and conversational, allowing anyone to reenter with new thoughts and inspirations.

At intervals of about once a month we agreed to celebrate the presence of the Lord in the sacrament of bread and wine. There was a feeling that to do this more frequently would tend to make it commonplace, and possibly rob the event of some of its deeper and fuller intent. This was always a very intimate and unifying experience. We began by meditating on the New Testament settings for the Lord's Supper, and sometimes turned back to the Passover origins in the book of Exodus. There was a wonderful feeling of "brother and sister" as we handed the broken loaf and the common chalice to each other. We always personalized this sharing of the sacramental elements—"Mike, this is the body of Christ, broken for you, so you can know your sins are forgiven." "Jill, this is the blood of Christ our Lord, shed for you, because of His love for you."

Apostolic Midwife

For a Church community to get started, to have a chance to grow, and before a local eldership can emerge, there is a critical need for some contemporary version of the "apostle." I have a feeling that he can be more succinctly conceived of as a sort of "midwife" whom the Holy Spirit has chosen to use in bringing the corporate body of Christ into a unique "birth," a recovery of the original Christian community. We have found that the capacity to turn from tradition to a New Testament concept of the Church involves a reorientation as radical as our initial entry into the family of faith! It is a significant second conversion, another mysterious "revelation" of the Holy Spirit.

Those who can break with tradition, and will search for new and meaningful forms of church life, tend to be individualists. And the one who is called to "bring to the light" (as Brazilians characterize birth), and to fuse the body of Christ into a functioning unit, will see the signs of bright promise and will sense the common immaturity that can lead to conflict. In this ferment of struggle and aspiration, the teaching of the Word and the ways of the Spirit is a continuing challenge.

Collective Potential

The teaching task is vastly simplified where everyone agrees that this is the exclusive prerogative of one talented "king pin" preacher. But in any such situation the content of the teaching is correspondingly limited. One who has attempted to do this "professionally" is conscious that, no matter how diligently he may study and prepare, his general effectiveness will tend to run in cycles. He discovers that he is probably "on target" and actually communicating about one Sunday out of four!

To me this intimates that something is out of orbit. Some "higher order" is quietly insisting that there are others out there in the silent assembly whom the Spirit has given a gift and a message. What a pity and what a loss when it lies dormant and undiscovered! So the modern midwife-apostle will pray that he may generate an approach to vital teaching that will call forth the collective potential of the brotherhood.

A midwife is on hand to render indispensable assistance in bringing to birth, stays long enough to assure that the baby will survive—then travels on to offer help in other localities. A like mobility may be required of today's "apostle," and may be equally essential to the growth and the learning of a Christian community. I think it is generally true that only when the Spirit-led initiator does move on, will the emerging leadership he has nurtured begin to function as it should. Certainly he will have to have the capacity to "sit loose" toward the local church if he is to headquarter in that vicinity.

Positive Traditions

The early Christians drew benefit from their Hebrew background, and I believe we can profit from the valid learnings of traditional churches. Everything of the past need not be discarded. I think of two contributions that can expand our consciousness of Kingdom life.

1. *The observance of the Church Year.* Following the colorful "seasons" of the Church Year, from Advent through Epiphany and Easter and Pentecost, can offer an attractive "highway" for the contem-

porary Church to follow. It provides the intervals and turn signals that comprise the major scenes on the redemption road.

2. *Some form of the pericope*[27] can also enhance the teaching perspective in the Christian assembly. Where the elders agree on sequential selections from the Old Testament, the Gospels and the Epistles, and where the members will commit themselves to daily meditation on these scriptures, there will almost certainly be items to share when they come together for worship. Recognizing (and admitting) the inborn inclination to rely on the leadership to "come through" in any case, it becomes a practical necessity for these elders to be especially prepared! After the selected scriptures have been heard, the invitation should invariably be given— to tell whatever the Spirit has spoken through the Word during the week. And I should think that the recurring opportunity would eventually prod the most reluctant and lethargic into participation.

If we have been negative toward the tradition of a general "pericope," it is because we have reacted against a lock-step rigidity that can also stifle. In the use of commonly selected scripture, it is important to emphasize the freedom to range beyond these selections for personal inspiration, and for possible expression in worship.

Model in Seattle

An ongoing lay community in Seattle, Washington, has discovered a worship and teaching pattern that is the most satisfactory of any I have observed. The members gather for an hour of meditational-type worship, interspersed with songs, expressions of praise, and spontaneous prayer. It closes with the Lord's Supper.

This is a "family affair," and is followed by a coffee break (with kool-aid for the kids). Then the children go into classes while the parents and singles get a solid hour of teaching, generally led by one or more of the elders. Everyone understands that it is a two-part package. There is no general exodus following worship, and no need for some sparsely attended "mid-week Bible study."

Adaptability and Commitment

The success of any venture to move into new and unexplored territory will hinge heavily on adaptability and commitment. Very few completed buildings will reflect every detail of the original blueprint. When the architect brings the prospective client a blueprint, he knows this may be merely the starting point. But it does get illusive dreams and ideas into a structure that can be realized. Along the way to completion, architect and client will both adapt and give ground—or there will be no building!

Like the early Christians, we can take some of our cues from where we have been. We will give respectful attention to the principles in the book of Acts. We will profit from the sometimes painfully acquired maturity of contemporary experiments in lay worship. But the ultimate ingredient will be commitment—the unconditional commitment of brothers and sisters—to stand by each other, no matter what! And it will mean commitment to a dream of New Community that can be better than the old.

Notes

1. Jeremiah 2:13 (NEB).
2. Acts 18:24-26 (NIV).
3. Luke 6:45 (NIV).
4. "Where two or three come together in my name, there am I with them" (Matt. 18:20, NIV). Can we come up with a better definition of the Church than the one Jesus has given us in these words?
5. John 4:19-24.
6. I Corinthians 5:19-13.
7. Ephesians 4:5, 6 (TEV).
8. I Corinthians 3:16 (NIV).
9. Romans 12:4-8; I Corinthians 12:12-30.
10. Acts 14:21; Acts 20:17 and 28; I Peter 5:1, 2.
11. Paul's flat statement to the Church at Corinth (I Cor. 14:34, 35) has to be reconciled with the comprehensive application we are given in his letter to the Church at Galatia (Gal. 3:36-39).
12. Acts 2:46 (NEB).

13. Ephesians 5:18-20 (NIV).

14. Colossians 3:16 (NIV).

15. Deuteronomy 11:18, 19 (NASB).

16. Luke 2:52 (TEV).

17. I John 2:16 (TEV).

18. I Corinthians 2:14 (Phillips).

19. Matthew 25:31-40 (Phillips).

20. Genesis 4:10.

21. John 17:16.

22. Matthew 6:33 (TEV).

23. I Peter 2:9 (NIV).

24. We have a current example of this in the statement dealing with biblical inerrancy in the Lausanne Covenant. Section 2 of the Covenant states that the Bible is "without error in all that it affirms. . . ." Intended to be a safeguard against liberal deviations, it apparently opens the door to other interpretations (*Eternity Magazine*, page 7, April 1975 issue).

25. Perhaps we should also point out that following a New Testament formula for the operation of the Church does not guarantee that there will be life! We can know all about the new wineskins of the Kingdom without having tasted the new wine which alone can make the Church come alive.

26. Acts 26:19, 20 (NIV).

27. Scripture selections to be read as a part of a liturgical worship service.

10

77 01693 224